A Walk
In The Park

Jonathan Chadwick

Published in the United Kingdom by

Vobster Press

vobsterpress@gmail.com

First published in 2013

This edition published in 2017 by Vobster Press

ISBN 978-1-9998310-0-4

TO JEN

who, despite all this, became my wife.

CONTENTS

Jonathan Chadwick

PROLOGUE

"Are you going up Kilimanjaro?" asked Rodney, one of my colleagues at work. "I grew up there."

"Did you?" I replied.

"Yes, I went up the mountain on a school trip when I was four."

"Four?" I must have sounded a little incredulous.

"Well, we drove two-thirds of the way up in a Land Rover. If you live there it's just one of the things you do."

"You went up Kilimanjaro when you were 4?"

A few others around the office were now listening in on the conversation.

"You don't believe me, do you? I can remember it clearly, our teacher driving us up and we were all bouncing around in the back, then we walked to the top and drove back."

"In a day?"

"Yeah, I think so."

"You think so? We're camping for 5 nights but you can stay in huts if you go a different route. Maybe you stayed overnight in some posh huts you thoughts were hotels?"

"No, I don't remember that. I think we did it on a day trip. It really wasn't that big a deal."

"It was definitely Kilimanjaro?"

"Yes! There's only one mountain. I went to Arusha International School. Look it up when you are there."

"Let me get this straight. You climbed Kilimanjaro on a school daytrip in your romper-suit when you were four years old and I'm taking 6 days with what I'm told is a 50% chance that I won't make

it due to altitude sickness and a once-a-month chance that I'll die?"
"If you don't believe me …"

ARRIVING IN AFRICA

Nairobi, capital city of Kenya. Once the capital of the British East Africa Protectorate, it was a city of grand hotels packed full with big game hunting ex-pats. Gentlemen called Toby and Miles carried elephant guns and dressed in safari suits and pith helmets. Ladies called Betsy and Camilla wore long, flowing cotton dresses and carried frilly umbrellas to shade themselves from the sun. Each day the men would venture into the jungle to bag some sport, ably assisted by a troupe of natives carrying their vast array of luggage along the narrow footpaths. The women would remain in the town, lounging on balconies and penning letters home complaining of the dastardly heat. The evenings were a long series of white tie balls in which champagne cocktails were popped and marital beds were hopped. Independence from British rule and the passing of a few decades might have made its mark but, in our brief time in the city, I expected to see the decaying remnants of another era.

Maybe I was a little naïve. Maybe I was the victim of watching too many BBC period dramas of the White Mischief variety as a child. Maybe I should have bought a guide book before booking to stay an extra night on the way back as well as the way there.

Nairobi today is a concrete copy of the worst of the modern Western cities it aspires to be, with a busy attitude and south bank skyline that belies its central African location. It houses some 2½ million people, although 'house' is perhaps the wrong word; almost a million live in Kibera slum, the largest slum in Africa. Crime is a constant and increasing problem, earning the city the unfortunate nickname "Nairobbery". The pollution has to be breathed to be believed; there is no tram, tube or local train system to speak of, so commuters use the numerous unroadworthy, badly driven and heavily polluting matutu buses. And just when you think that there can't be many more things going against the city you find out that it is a very real terrorist target. Nairobi suffered one of the worst terrorist attacks in recent times when, on 7 August 1998, a truck bomb destroyed the US Embassy, killing 224 people and injuring 4000 more. The perpetrators belonged to a then relatively unknown organisation called al Qaeda.

On the positive side, due to its 1660m altitude Nairobi enjoys a relatively cool climate for a city this close to the equator. Even at the warmest in February and March the temperatures barely reach 26C. At the coolest, in July, temperatures can sink to as low as 10C (when you can also expect 1.5cm of rain). Not at all what a naïve and perhaps a little under-prepared Brit might imagine arriving from London in a city 90 miles south of the equator.

It is on a chilly and overcast July day that a naïve Brit and his girlfriend Jenny, dressed in a t-shirt, shorts and donning a sun-hat, took his first steps onto the continent of Africa. We're here with one main aim: to climb to the top of the world's tallest, free-standing mountain, Kilimanjaro.

The overnight flight from Heathrow to Nairobi had been remarkable only for the unexplained disappearance of Jenny's inflatable pillow. We'd bought the pillow while waiting for our flight, succumbing as we all do to the lure of buying something we don't need in the duty free shops, under the pretence that it really would be useful, that it will be used on future holidays as well as this one, and that it really is such a bargain. The persuasiveness of the buy-one-get-one-half-price stickers makes the average traveller forget that they didn't really want even one in the first place let alone a second at a price that only looks favourable compared to the overpriced first. On a previous trip we had sniggered at a fellow passenger with an inflatable pillow, ear plugs and eye shades and marveled at just how much essential traveller paraphernalia you can end up lugging around if you're not ruthless about your packing. A little inflatable pillow here (why not roll up your t-shirt around your neck?), an extra pair of knickers in case of emergencies there (if you have an emergency, don't wear any), satellite navigation (we paid for a guided tour … with a guide …

who will guide us … didn't we?). Each a little thing in itself, yet the size and weight of the whole quickly feels greater than the sum of the parts. Only a fool doesn't see this.

Or so we'd discussed and smugly agreed. Back at Heathrow and in full pre-holiday stupor, Jen and I were idly browsing through the racks of essentialities with our rational armour firmly in place.

"Ooh, look at this pillow! It's all furry."

"Aw, isn't that nice."

"Feel it, it's like a cat."

"Ha, yes, you could stroke it while you went to sleep."

And so the conversation gently ambled along its way until Jen said

"I think I'll get one"

and I replied

"Why not, we're on holiday!"

Wham! The curse of Duty Free shopping had struck. And once it strikes, it can really take a hold.

"Look", I continued, "we only have one travel plug with us, which might not be enough. If we get one of those as well, we can get something else free."

"But we don't need anything else", said Jen.

"Good point. All the travel stuff is just crap anyway, and these chocolates that are also in the deal would only make us fat."

We looked at each other.

"Yay, we're on holiday!" we cried.

Duty Free? More like Guilt Free and even more like Brain Free.

So, as with all duty free purchases, we put them to use as soon as possible to prove what an excellent buy they were, what clever people we were to buy them and how cool we are with them. Although the travel plug will have to wait until Nairobi, a chocolate helps with take-off (it's the sucking, apparently) and the wrapping is off the pillow immediately after the meal has been cleared away. As I said, the flight was remarkable only for the pillow cat's disappearance. Jenny went to sleep in a window seat with it around her neck. I dozed off next to her with my jumper around my neck. (I'm a real man, after all.) When we woke up in the morning the cat pillow was gone.

After a good deal of searching and eventual resignation that it had mysteriously disappeared, Jenny miserably trudged off to the toilet. As I sat down I spotted a similar cat pillow around the neck of a woman in the centre seat of the aisle in front. Similar or the same one, I wondered? Clearly there was quite a high chance she had also bought a pillow in the same Duty Free shop. It was such a good deal, you will recall. How would she have stolen it anyway, and who would have the nerve to steal it and then use it on the plane in front of us? Maybe she had just picked it up and then used it? If I had found it on the floor, would I have held on to it? Even if I had kept it, I thought to myself, would I have slept on it? Probably not. Maybe I should just ask her if she'd "found it". The payoff would have been big hugs from Jen and smiles all round. The risk was that the thief said it was hers. Surely she wouldn't? It was clearly our pillow. But the thief was asleep. I was sure it was our pillow though. I couldn't see any others on the flight, so it must have been. I was convinced.

The woman stirred awake as the man next to her stood up and went to join the toilet queue. It provided an ideal opportunity to ask her. She stretched and put the cat pillow down on the seat next to her.

Aha! In an instant I saw it all. That must be what happened. Jen must have flopped over me in the night and the pillow dropped onto the floor. Someone then picked it off the floor and placed it onto the empty seat next to the woman. The woman saw it, assumed it was owned by her friend next to her and borrowed it. Her friend returned, thought it was her pillow and neither commented on where it came from. Mystery solved, except that the cat pillow was still on the seat over there. There was only one thing to do: steal it back.

To make the one thing that bit easier, the woman stretched again and also headed off for the toilet. I nipped down, grabbed our cat pillow and was back in my seat before she'd reached the toilet queue. A quick look at the pillow and, well, unless they had bought an absolutely identical pillow it was definitely ours. There really couldn't be two like this little feller.

"Aw, you've found it!" Jen said as she arrived back from the toilet.

"Yup." I was pretty pleased with myself and explained all the detective work and super-sleuthing that had gone on while she'd been away. I could see she was torn between knowing I was probably right and that we'd got the cat pillow back and knowing I could be wrong and that we'd stolen someone else's pillow. When did this pillow become so important to either of us?

"Let's see what they say when they get back", I offered. "If they start to hunt around for it, I'll ask them if it's theirs."

We both anxiously awaited their return. The man returned first and sat down. The woman then arrived back and did the same. Neither showed any sign of missing their pillow, so we were both satisfied. For good measure, I kept an eye on them for the rest of the flight and they never appeared to notice anything missing. Proof at last. Proof enough, anyway.

I now wonder if they ever discovered that neither of them owned a cat pillow. Do they ever wonder where their beautiful furry pillow appeared from one night over Africa, only to disappear into the morning mist the following day?

The next time we went to use the cat pillow, on the flight home, we found that it had developed a puncture and was unusable. My mum would call it divine retribution. I called it typical Duty Free rubbish. Jen wants to get another one.

Our first footsteps on African tarmac are cold ones. Even accounting for the early morning and lack of good sleep, it is cold. By the time we pass through passport control we are wearing jumpers and the coats we've brought to wear at the top of Kilimanjaro, the mountain we are here to climb. We take a taxi to our hotel, the Silver Springs.

Our tour starts properly tomorrow morning with a bus ride from Nairobi to Moshi, so we have just under 24 hours to fill. It's about 8.30am when we arrive at the hotel where we're told it's too early to check in. We leave our bags at the reception and head to the bar for some water and a coffee.

The hotel is built around a central, open-air swimming pool. The bar is on one side, the breakfast room is opposite and the reception area is at the poolside between the two. We sit at a table in the reception area.

We booked the trip in January as an organised tour, starting and ending at this hotel in Nairobi. The flights were a separate booking. Many tours like this one are built up from components a week or so long. For us, we start with the 6-day walk up Kilimanjaro (plus travel to and from) and finish with a second week on safari in the Ngorogoro Crater, Serengeti and Lake Manyara National Parks. The safari feels like a lifetime away given what we've got to attempt first. The trip is a compromise, a mixture of the holiday we both want. I have been keen to climb Kilimanjaro for a number of years and am interested in going on safari. Jen has always wanted to do a safari and sees climbing Kili as a feat that would be an achievement to have done. An optional extra was a third week in Zanzibar, which we declined because it's too expensive in terms of both time and money and fundamentally it's not really why either of us is going on this trip. We're also too fidgety to be good beach-holiday people.

The component-structure means that people join and leave the tour along the way, so your starting companions may not be your finishing ones. The fact that the flights are not a part of the tour means that, although there are almost certainly others here at the hotel that will be on our tour, we do not yet know who they are. We find ourselves in a people-watching, speculating frame of mind, trying to imagine our travel companions and conscious that they may ultimately help or hinder our success. From our seats we can see people coming down from their rooms to breakfast, as well as those arriving at and leaving the hotel. Breakfast looks extensive, with an array of cooked meats, cooked vegetables, breads, cereals, yoghurts and fruits. We're tempted despite (or maybe because of) having eaten on the plane, so to reduce our salivating we start guessing who else might be joining us on the tour. While Jenny is keen that she's not the only girl, I'm looking for people with bigger bellies who should be less fit. Neither of us wants to be the one to hold the group back or be the only one not to make it to the top of Kili.

We both trawled the internet and read a few guide books before we came and also spoke to a couple of friends who'd attempted the climb. The chances of reaching the top are just 50:50 (depending on which book or internet site you read) and are supposedly not helped by any of the usual physical advantages of fitness, youth or masculinity. Although we accept this to some degree, experience tells us that, on average, a fat old woman is likely to find any hill harder to climb than a thin young man, regardless of the altitude sickness lottery that could strike either of them. Neither of us wants to be the fattest, oldest or girliest. I win on masculinity while Jen wins on age. Neither of us is fat.

The "Who's on the tour?" game throws up four likely candidates and any number of possibles. A couple of twenty-something boys who look pretty lean head the list and a couple of twenty-something girls come a close second. Jen has high hopes that the girls are on the tour. So have I; not because they're hot but because one of them has a decent belly on her. There are a few families at breakfast, none of whom look like they'll be walking up a mountain in the near future, and a few singles who don't look like walkers but could be on a 'trip of a lifetime' experience. As for the rest, the only mountain they're likely to tackle is the mountain of food they've piled onto their plate for breakfast. As a general rule, if your belly button enters the room before your nipples, you're probably not fit enough to climb Kili.

Although we could ask any of them if they are on our tour – they too are lazing around waiting for their rooms – we adopt the default British position and don't say anything.

At ten o'clock I check back with reception and our room is available. It's a perfectly adequate double room that doesn't appear to have been refurbished in many years although nor does it really need to be. We shower and test the bed and note that the plug sockets are of the British 3-pin variety with no need for an adaptor.

By 1.30pm we are up and deep in negotiations with the lady on the entry desk to the hotel spa.

"So if I want to have a Jacuzzi I need to come back at four o'clock?" I clarified.

Having dismissed the outdoor pool due to the inclement temperature, we'd thought that an hour in the indoor pool would do wonders to perk us up. However it appears that there are single-sex bathing rules and it's women only until 4pm.

"If there is no-one in there right now then you can go in now, but if anyone else comes along then you'll have to leave," said the spa attendant.

Although there is no mixed bathing, we finally appear to have reached a compromise.

"Ah, so let's do that, two for the Jacuzzi then and we'll take the risk of losing our money if someone comes along."

"No, no, you can go in if she" pointing at Jen "waits outside. Then she can go in when you get out."

"We've seen each other naked before. I promise that I won't

blush when she gets in."

The attendant smiles, patiently.

"I'll promise to refrain from any naughty stuff?" I add in a last ditched attempt but it still isn't to be. Not wanting a tag-team spa, we go back to our room and change for a walk into town instead.

The hotel is in the suburbs of the city, a couple of miles from the centre. We dither and debate whether or not we should walk into town or get a taxi. We'd prefer to walk, as a practice for what is to come if nothing else. However it is not the sort of city to find yourself in the wrong place. It's not as if we have any chance of blending in with the locals and, although the environs of the hotel look decent enough and the centre will no doubt be fine, we have no idea about the area in between. I check at reception. The lady on the desk is sure that it is safe but would like to check with her colleague. Her colleague is also sure, as long as we stick to the main road, but she would like to ask the manager for the final say. The manager is sure too, as long as we are back before dark. I'm pleased that they are all so sure because I'm not any more. We walk anyway.

The level of air pollution has to be breathed to be believed. The hotel is on a small hill above the city centre and the road takes a straight path down. It's not a steep slope by any measure but it is enough to make the matutu, the small local buses, shift into a lower gear and grind slowly upwards. As they do the gear shift and accelerate they disappear behind a thick black cloud of exhaust smoke that belches out and covers the pavement. Our noses tingle and our eyes sting. We are caught by a belch and momentarily lose the ability to breathe. After the fumes from the second bus nearly knock us over, we hold our noses and close our eyes as soon as a matutu nears. I'm sure it's not a safe thing to do.

Coming from a city in Western Europe, it's easy to take for granted how clean our air actually is. Londoners may complain about the air pollution levels at the height of summer but everything is relative. It may not be as fresh as the Welsh hills (which can be fresh in their own way) but relative to Nairobi we do very well indeed.

It takes half an hour to reach what we assume is the city centre, a collection of shabby shops glued together with concrete. There is no focal point. There appears to be nothing to see. No beautiful and run-down buildings to admire. No nice squares to relax in. We find the Hilton, a concrete hotel with less shabby shops and a doorman. The parliament buildings are just buildings with a lot of flags outside.

We find a supermarket and buy a few snacks for our dinner later. We're intrigued by the chocolate counter, which has Cadbury's versions of Bounty, Twix, Snickers and Mars Bars. Clearly we need to try them all.

We consider stocking up for the trek and decide to do that once we arrive in Moshi or even at the start of the trail. When I walked the Inca Trail last year there were numerous opportunities to buy chocolate bars such as Snickers, right down to women thrusting them at you as you set foot on the trail. We only have limited Kenyan Schillings as most of the tour will be spent in Tanzania, so we buy enough food for this evening and plan to get more on the way.

Having exhausted the tourist traps, we head for something to eat at the Thorn Tree Café, the famous "centre of Nairobi". The café is a part of the Stanley Hotel, built in 1902 as Nairobi's first hotel. It was originally built to house railway staff and trains actually stopped right outside for people to get on and off. The train line has long disappeared and the hotel has moved upmarket (in clientele, at least), catering for princes, presidents and prime ministers during its history. The Acacia thorn tree was planted in 1959 to provide shade for the outdoor tables of the hotel café and became famous as travellers posted messages and letters on its trunk. The café was a great meeting point sheltered from the bustle of downtown Nairobi and, at its peak, the base of the tree was surrounded by a notice board covered in messages. Lonely Planet even calls their online notice board The Thorn Tree.

The modern-day Thorn Tree café is indeed a haven from Nairobi, if only offering an escape from the omni-present pollution. The outside tables are thankfully more inside than out, although there is an opening in the glass roof. The famous tree, though, is rather squibby and I suspect that it might be an offcut of the great original. The notice board is also a poor reflection of its former glory – it's just a small board set to one side of the tree and with very few postings. The notice board is no doubt a victim of internet email. After all, why pin a letter to a tree and hope one of your friends might pass by and read it when you can more easily type an email in one of the many internet shops or send a mobile phone text from anywhere and have the added bonus that it will reach your friend with almost 100% certainty? It's private too, so if you want to whinge about that girl with the annoying voice on your last trip then there's less of a danger of her reading it. (Although if she does read it she'll know exactly who said what, as many of my university friends learnt when the group email discussion about whether or not "Tammy 'tache" shaved was accidentally forwarded to Tammy. It was a pointless discussion anyway. She clearly didn't shave.)

We buy a couple of pizzas, a coke and a lemonade. It's perfectly edible but nothing to stick a note to the tree about. We pay and leave to have one last attempt at seeing something noteworthy in the centre of Nairobi. We find the Hilton and parliament again and give up. We're unsure what time the sun sets, which is a slight concern to me. My only concept of an equatorial sunset is from a Lenny Henry sketch many years ago: "One moment you're walking through a field in the afternoon sunshine then the next, before anyone can say NIGHT! the sun's disappeared and there are all sorts of horrible noises going on." I don't want to be caught out, so we walk back to the hotel.

The slog back up the hill is even more polluted than the walk down. It's now rush hour and there is far more traffic. Remarkably, the matutu buses are even fuller, so they struggle even more to climb the hill. The matutus have seats for about 25 people and are easily carrying twice that. Young men cling on to the outside. Small children sit on the windscreen ledge. Large women appear to be sitting on top of each other.

Due to the lack of oxygen we also struggle, no doubt a taste of things to come. We finally wheeze into the hotel and call at the bar to see if they will be showing the Germany vs Argentina World Cup quarter final. They are, and on a big screen too, we are assured. We use the time until kick-off to have a shower to get rid of the pollution, which washes out of our hair like stale smoke the morning after a night out clubbing.

The big screen is a stippled wall lit by a projector. The quality is surprisingly good, much better than trying to peer at a small screen in some London pubs. The bar has enough people interested in the game to make an atmosphere of sorts. The game, on the other hand, is very poor. We survive a first half of midfield mistakes and no shots on goal and decide to watch the second half in bed. We had considered eating in the bar but the option of our fake chocolate bars and a couple of bottles of British Airways red wine win over against Chicken Gordon Blue and BEST (Bacon, Eggs, Sausage and Tomato) and chips.

The game isn't covered by the set of channels on the TV in our room. Neither of us can be bothered to go back down to the bar, so we scoff our chocolate, down the wine and fall asleep.

In Berlin, the game kicked into life with a goal from Argentina 4 minutes into the second half. Germany went on to equalise and then win the game on penalties after a goalless extra time. German goalkeeper Lehman saved the two missed Argentinian penalties that won the game.

In Hamburg an hour later, Italy comfortably beat Ukraine 3-0. They will meet Germany in the semi-final. We slept through that game too.

SCHOOLBOY ERROR

There may be lies, damned lies and statistics, yet in the case of Wales' forays into World Cup football there are truths, frustrating truths and statistics that back it all up. The truth is that there has been only one campaign, Sweden 1958. The frustrating truths are dotted with missed chances; Joe Jordan deliberately handballing in the Welsh area and gaining a Scottish penalty taking them to Argentina '78; Paul Bodin's missed penalty against Romania for USA '94; not to mention the drugs tests and disallowed goals that have ensured failure to ever reach the European Championships. The statistics show that, of the 5 games in Sweden, Wales won one, drew three and lost one. The loss was in the quarter finals, a one-nil defeat to the champions-in-waiting Brazil. The goal was the first World Cup goal scored by the single most famous player in World Cup history – Edson Arantes do Nascimento, or Pele as he was soon to be known.

England, on the other hand, have reached the final stages in 12 of the 15 World Cups that they have entered, winning 25 of the 55 games played, reaching the quarter finals on 6 occasions, the semi finals once and famously winning in '66.

We've chosen to come to Africa during the latter stages of the FIFA World Cup, which is taking place in Germany. The group stages and first knock-out round finished while we were still in London. Next it's the quarter finals. England are playing Portugal tomorrow night, at 6pm, on the eve of our Kilimanjaro climb. If they progress we will miss their semi-final and who knows where we'll be for the final. Why, you may ask, have two football fans placed themselves in such a predicament?

It's a good question and one that merits a good answer.

Firstly, I'm not English. I'm Welsh, and the fact that I'm Welsh is an important part of the answer. I was born in Bangor, North Wales and grew up on Holy Island, a little island off Anglesey, which in turn is a slightly bigger island just off the North Wales coast. It sounds much more idyllic than it is in reality (sorry Mum). Holy Island is connected to Anglesey by a road bridge, a road/rail causeway and a whopping concrete dual carriageway flyover. Anglesey is connected to North Wales by two bridges, a beautiful suspension bridge for road traffic built in 1826 by Thomas Telford and a more functional railway bridge built in 1850 by Robert Stephenson. In 1980 the railway had a roadway slung over the top of it, finally allowing cars to enter and leave the island more quickly than a horse and cart. Most travellers through (and many people do travel through rather than to) are probably unaware that they have left the mainland when they arrive in Holyhead, the main town and ferry port for Ireland.

Llaingoch is a village just outside Holyhead at the base of Holyhead Mountain, a 220m high hill not even one-twenty-sixth the height of Kili. It's not actually a very high hill and it takes only 20 minutes to walk to the top from my gran's house at the bottom. A little known fact is that it is an official Marilyn (defined as a hill in the British Isles that is more than 500 feet higher than the surrounding area). The term Marilyn must have been coined as a counterpart to the Munro, a Scottish mountain over 3000 feet in height. Having just looked it up (on Google, where else) there appears to be a whole list of names for hills meeting various criteria of absolute or relative height (Munros, Corbetts, Donalds and Nuttalls to name a few). The groups mostly seem to be named by people who want to climb all hills meeting certain criteria. There are currently 1554 Marilyns in the British Isles (the list is sometimes updated when new maps are issued with revised heights for peaks and valleys) with 3 people claiming to have climbed 1549. The map (Google is great, isn't it?) shows 5 dots well into the Atlantic. Now I wonder which ones they've yet to complete …

Like many of my generation, leaving school coincided with leaving Holyhead. I went to university and then got a job after a (then more unusual) gap year spent volunteering in Doncaster. I now live in London and love it.

The next important part of the answer is that, in contrast to me, Jenny is English. She was born in Kettering, brought up in Leighton Buzzard and now lives in south London. Until I met Jen, Leighton Buzzard was one of those places with a bizarre name that no-one you ever meet ever comes from. Think Hemel Hempstead, Saffron Walden or Aberystwyth and you'll get the idea. (The name doesn't have as exotic an origin as it sounds. No history of mysterious falconry here. The 12th century Dean of Lincoln had two Leightons (or forest clearings) in his diocese and to distinguish between the two simply added the name of his local rep in the area, Theobald de Busar.)

In no particular order, Jen is lively, funny, blonde, willing to give most things a go, scared of spiders, slightly clumsy and exactly the sort of travelling companion you dream about. Whatever she does, you know it will be fun. However bad things might appear, she'll make sure we have the best possible time. We've been on a few trips of varying lengths and invariably had a great time. We almost never do what we plan and always seem to do something that seems even better.

Our first trip together was a weekend in Dublin, where we came away as accidental but big fans of the Galway hurling team. On the Sunday we were due to fly home, we'd decided to spend a cultured afternoon in the James Joyce centre. We arrived at the address we'd been given by our hotel receptionist to find a normal house with no indication that there was any museum or centre. We walked down the street and found a sign that sent us back the way we came. We followed it, past the house we'd started at and ended up at the other end of the street, next to another sign sending us back where we'd just come from. We tried this one more time, examining every house closely in case the centre was a discreet affair. No luck, we simply arrived at the previous sign. Flummoxed, we stood hands on hips and stared at the sign like bewildered tourists. A little man, no taller than Jen, who is five feet and three-quarters of an inch tall, came up to us. He had a few days growth of beard, unwashed hair and a generally unkempt appearance. There was a definite air of shiftiness about him.

"Doi yer wan' a ticket foir de goime?" he asked.

We pretended to not hear. Although I was grateful that he wasn't begging, I had the feeling that my wallet was about to find a new owner.

"Shall we try this way?" I asked Jen, turning around and pointing in the opposite direction to the man.

"Oi'm sellin' at cost, yer know", said the little man.

"What game?" asked Jen in the innocent way that she has.

"De foinal o' the hurlin'! Toirty-foive euros each, cost proice. Oi'm makin' nuttin' orn de ticket, moiself."

He showed us the tickets and they looked genuine, complete and indeed had a price of €35 in the corner.

"I don't know what hurling is" laughed Jen.

"Aw, loike hockey only roofer! Tis de foinal. Yer'll luvit, yer will. Yer'll tank me fer the rest yer loife. De best game der is."

I was tempted. The game was at Croke Park, which I knew would be an exciting stadium in which to see the game, and it sounded much more fun than a mouldy old literary centre that we couldn't even find. I looked at Jen. She was tempted too.

"Toirty-five euros, cost proice", the man repeated.

"Shall we do it?" Jen asked to me.

"Let's do it", I said.

So we paid the little man our seventy euros and we took our tickets. He scampered off rather sharply, if not a little too sharply for my liking. I looked more closely at the tickets. They seemed genuine enough, certainly not counterfeit. And the price … hmmm. The three looked suspiciously like it was a late addition with a ballpoint pen. Looking even closer, I could see the indentation of the pen confirming that we'd just paid seven times the asking price for the tickets.

"Oh well", said Jen, as the con became clear. "It's done now. We might as well go to the game anyway."

So go to the game we did. Along the way we found a stall selling braids in the team colours. There were four colours of braid, which the stall owner explained were the colours of the four teams playing. Four teams? That's right, he replied, two teams in each of the quarter-finals playing today. Quarter-final? I checked the tickets but they didn't specify. By now I knew who to believe and it wasn't our little ticket seller. While I pondered how I could have been conned so completely and whether the con would be complete by us not getting into the ground at all, Jen was more concerned with choosing a braid-colour for a team that was both in the first game (in case we had to leave early for the airport) and a nice colour. She chose burgundy and white, which happened to be the colours of Galway.

Thankfully the tickets were genuine and we were able to watch the game. (On the way we passed the queue for tickets at the ground and realised that we could have bought them at cost.) The game was tremendous, very exciting and a closely-fought battle between Galway and Tipperary (I think – I can't actually remember). We loved it and made sure that we watched the semi-final (Galway won again) and final (Galway lost, bah) in an Irish bar in London.

One final amusing moment was as we left to make sure we caught our flight. As suspected, we were only able to stay to see the first game and a few minutes of the second. We walked away from the ground as fans were arriving late for the second game. One group of teenage male fans saw Jen's colours and started chanting loudly and waving their Limerick flags at us. Jen, more used to football crowds, was genuinely scared and looked to me for help. As if I knew what to do!

Fortunately the boys noticed how scared she was.

"No, no, we didn't moin to froighten ye! Sorry, sorry, sorry!" they shouted and backed off, waving their hands in apology. They carried on past, blowing kisses at Jen, apologising and laughing all the way.

Having paid seven times cost price, not for a final, we could easily have felt pretty peeved with our final afternoon in Dublin. On the other hand, as we reasoned it, if we hadn't paid that much we wouldn't have seen the game at all or become hurling fans. We'd have probably just spent the afternoon in the pub. The event set a tone for much of our travel ever since: plan for one thing, do another, and enjoy it even more than we thought we'd enjoy the planned event.

The final part of the answer to the question of exactly how we have found ourselves in Africa during the World Cup finals with a distinct chance of not being able to watch any games from the quarter finals onwards is that we booked the holiday in January. In January, the World Cup was a June thing. Everyone talked about watching the games in June. Even the BBC was advertising it (6 months in advance) as a June event. No-one mentioned that, actually, the games only started in June and finished a good way into July. As a Welshman and therefore neutral World Cup supporter, I had no need to check such details. Of course I would be supporting England (I do live there after all) but not to the extent that I have a wallchart on my bedroom wall and all the games scheduled in my diary.

Jenny, on the other hand, is English and a big football fan. I relied on her patriotism and fanaticism and assumed she'd know if we were booking the holiday over the finals. She relied on my masculinity – "a boy should just know these things" – and assumed that I would know if we were booking a holiday over the finals. We didn't spot the mistake until May, when I was sent a computer file that put all the games in my work diary as "unavailable". It was only because I conscientiously went through every game and changed them to "available" that I noticed the latter games coincided with the trip.

"Bit of a schoolboy error", joked one of our friends at us.

"See, schoolboy error. SchoolBOY error", said Jen.

"Bovvered", I shrugged.

"You will be if we get to the final and we're on some mountainside without a telly. I just won't go up the mountain", she joked.

At least, I think she was joking.

It certainly adds an extra dimension to the trip. If England win tomorrow night, the semi-final will kick-off barely four hours before we attempt the final climb to the summit of Kilimanjaro. Winning or losing the game will undoubtedly affect the mood and therefore potentially even whether we succeed or fail. In many ways it may be easier if England lose in the quarter-finals. It will certainly be less of a distraction and one less unknown factor. I suspect that such a thought is unlikely to go down well in the present company and keep quiet.

Anyway, first things first. We still have to be in Moshi by 6pm so that we can watch the quarter-final game. Nairobi to Moshi in 10 hours? It should be a doddle.

THE DAY BEFORE THE FIRST DAY OF THE CLIMB

It makes sense, to me at least, to call the day of our first steps up the mountain Day One. Then the day before the big event is obviously Day-Minus-One, two days before is Day-Minus-Two, and so on. Simple and clear. But hold on a second, whatever happened to Day Zero? In any normal numbering system, the expected order is -2, -1, 0, 1, 2. To jump from -1 to 1 is missing out a whole number, which can't be right either. But Day Zero? What day is Day Zero? If Day One is the first day, it must be the day before the first day. So then it is Day Zero, not Day Minus One. Day Zero, therefore (and what a great mathematician's word "therefore" is), is in the set of days "before we set off". So this day is Day Zero. Happy? No, nor me. D-Day was effectively the first day of the campaign to liberate Europe in the Second World War. D-Day+1 was the second day. Day Zero was clearly in the set of days after things had got going.

The confusion arises from the use of numbers to define periods of time. A number is a point between minus infinity and infinity. A day, though, is not a point at all. It is a period of time between two points (midnight to midnight). Normally there is no confusion at all. It's only when zero gets involved that things get tricky. Zero is never a period between two points. It is always a point. We can all imagine spending one day doing something. Immediately there is a picture of a period of time in your head. Now picture spending no days doing something. What you imagine isn't a period any more.

Anyway, where does this leave the title of the chapter? Day Zero is confusing. Day Minus One isn't correct. The Day Before the First

Day of the Climb is both correct and clear. Hurrah! Success at last.
Let's ignore the fact that it's too long and aesthetically disagreeable.

We have an early start to make sure that there is time for breakfast before the Impala Shuttle leaves at 8am. I open the curtains to see 6 painters already working on the far wall of the hotel. It's another overcast day.

Although breakfast yesterday looked extensive and exciting, the reality today is a little disappointing. As a vegetarian all the meat options are off the menu, and I've decided to avoid fresh fruit and vegetables until we at least begin the walk, and to avoid dairy on the advice of a work colleague who didn't make it to the top. This leaves the selection of breads, toast and conserves, including croissants and doughnuts. They look good but are all stale. The bread would benefit from toasting except there is no toaster, the doughnuts have the texture of damp cardboard and the croissants taste furry inside. I spread on more jam, which helps. Given my fussiness I can hardly complain.

We are still playing the game of "Who's on our trip?". There's no sign of the two girls we saw last night and the two boys have eaten and gone already. The remaining breakfasters are not even candidates. They'll be lucky to walk to their taxis.

We head back to the room to collect our bags, check out from the hotel and wait for the shuttle. I leave Jen sitting on the floor in reception amidst our rucksacks and daysacks and wander out to see if the bus has arrived. The air is damp and rain feels imminent. The shuttle hasn't arrived and I return to find Jen in conversation with one of the two boys who were leading our "Who's on the tour?" game.

"Hi, I'm Andy", he says, standing up from the floor where he and Jen were sitting.

"Hi, Jon", I say.

"Another one. The guy I'm with is a John as well."

"Well, I'm a Jonathan really."

"So's he!"

"They're on our trip", says Jen.

"Cool."

John arrives and we repeat the Jon conversation. How polite we are.

"Cold, isn't it?" says Andy, who is wearing shorts and t-shirt. "I thought we were in Africa."

"It looks like it's about to rain too", says John.

Maybe we weren't so naïve after all.

Talk turns to the football game later on in the evening and whether or not we will arrive in Moshi in time for kick off at 6pm. John and Andy are keen to see the game too. Our itinerary says we will arrive mid afternoon and, even allowing for African time to turn into late afternoon, we should still be able to see the game.

"Impala shuttle?" A uniformed woman has opened the front door of the hotel and is looking at us.

"That's us", I say. Leaving on time is a good start if we are to make the game.

We load up our bags – Jen and I have far more stuff than the boys – and head outside and around the side of the hotel. The shuttle is a white minibus with a bustling crowd of a dozen or so people around it. A few people are sitting quietly inside. A man is on the roof of the minibus with a tarpaulin under his feet that is hanging down the side of the van. Various items of luggage are already on the roof and more litters the ground around the bus. We add our bags to the litter and find a seat on the bus. Inside, the seats are arranged with two on one side of the aisle and one on the other. Jen and I pick a two-seater, while Andy and John grab a single seat each. The passengers are a mixture of white and black faces. As I watch our bags being lifted onto the roof, a few spots of rain start to fall. So much for the dry season.

Our itinerary tells us to take the shuttle to Moshi, where we will be met by our Tour Leader and from where we will begin our ascent of Kilimanjaro. Moshi is in Tanzania, and we will cross the border with Kenya en route from Nairobi. The man on the roof finishes loading the bags, ties down the tarpaulin and jumps into the driver's seat. The doors shut and we leave the Silver Springs behind us. The bus isn't full, which is always good on a long journey. However, we stop at another hotel and collect a couple more Westerners before heading out of Nairobi. On the outskirts we stop again and collect a group of 6 Europeans who look like they've been dropped off straight from the airport. Our bus doesn't have 6 free seats so we assume they aren't joining us, but they all start to climb aboard nevertheless. Hidden at the end of each single seat is a fold-out seat that fills the aisle, and dropping these down provides for another 3 seats. Suddenly it's a very full bus. Another bus arrives with a group of South Africans. Surely there's no more room on our bus? I check above me to make sure there aren't any seats that drop down from the ceiling. Maybe they'll sit on our knees? The South Africans mill around for a while, getting on and off their bus and thankfully making no move to board ours. We leave before they do. Phew.

As we head off we realise that the Europeans are actually Portuguese. If they are staying in our hotel we'll have a fun evening tonight, and if they are in our group on the mountain then I can only hope England win.

The journey is quite slow and it's 3 hours before we take a break. It's the last stop before the border and it's a chance to go to the toilet and buy some African art. To get to the toilets you have to walk through the craft shop. The shop is floor to ceiling full of dark wooden animals, Masai warriors and weapons. A tower of 10-feet tall giraffes crowds next to a parade of elephants. Spears of all sizes are propped against a tribe of Masai warriors. Leopard spotted bowls with wildebeest spoons are filled with traditional bracelets and necklaces. There's no attempt to make the products have an air of exclusivity. This is African art, Wal-Mart style. In the toilets the hand-wash is a bottle of Head and Shoulders instead of soap. It works fine. We rejoin the bus and make the 5-minute trip to the border.

Even before we stop the bus is surrounded by craft sellers and sim-card vendors. A few others appear to be selling nothing at all but still want our money. We pile off the bus and head over to the Kenyan border office to queue for the exit stamp in our passports. We are given a yellow form and a white form, yellow to exit Kenya, white to enter Tanzania. We fill them both out while we queue.

The first step is easy enough, and Jen and I leave the Kenyan office with our exit stamps.

"Do we walk across to the Tanzanian side?" I ask Jen.

"Dunno", she replies.

"This way, I take you across to get Tanzania visa", says a man who has appeared at our side and has fallen in step with us. He is better dressed than most of the people around us, wearing a bright blue fleece and dark trousers. I ignore him, vaguely recognising him as being outside the bus when we got off.

"We've got visas, thanks", says Jen.

"OK", he says, "I take you to get the stamp."

"Stamp?" asks Jen.

"Entry stamp. This way."

"Is he one of the bus agents?" I whisper to Jen.

"He was at the bus when we arrived," she whispers back.

We walk towards the border and are about to cross when he guides us around a corner and into a small wooden shack about 6 feet square. There is a counter across the middle. One man is standing behind the counter, another is at the end of the counter. The man behind the counter has a clipboard and a list on it. He puts his pen to the list.

"Tanzania visa?"

"Entry stamp," says our blue-fleeced helper, who is standing in the doorway behind us.

"Passports?" asks the man with the list.

We have our passports in our hands. I'm feeling quite uneasy about this situation. I can sense that Jen is too. She looks uncertainly at me and I shrug. It doesn't seem right but then it doesn't seem wrong either. Jen hands her passport over.

"Entry stamp? Two persons. $100", says the man at the end of the counter.

He puts what looks like five 20,000 Tanzanian shilling notes into Jen's passport and hands it back to her.

He then looks at me, so I hand over my passport and get a similar number of Shillings back inside it. Any doubts I might have had a few moments ago have disappeared. This still seems a bit odd but at least we aren't being ripped off.

"$100", repeats the man behind the counter.

It appears that we have to exchange US$100 for the equivalent in Tanzanian Shillings before we cross the border, and then we'll actually pay for the visa in the official office.

Jen looks at me, shrugs and hands over the $100. The man behind the counter looks set to finish when the man at the end of the counter looks at me and says "$100 each".

"Each?" I say.

"$100 each."

Quickly working out that the 100,000 Tanzanian shillings nestling inside my passport that I am holding converts to about US$100, I also hand over a folded $100 bill to the man behind the counter. He takes the money and puts it in his pocket, rubbing it between his thumb and forefinger as he did so.

"You have visas?" he says, suddenly.

"They have visas", shouts the blue fleeced helper behind us.

"They have visas?" exclaims the man at the end of the counter.

"They have visas, they have visas!" proclaims the man behind the counter.

Amidst much laughing and repeating that we have visas, he hands back the $100 bills to both of us and asks for the shillings back. We oblige amidst much amusement that we have all been through this charade for nothing. Our blue fleeced helper guides us out of the hut and back onto the main thoroughfare. Jen and I look at each other.

"We're lucky not to have been completely conned there", I say.

"I know", laughs Jen. "What are we like?"

"Idiots, that's what. We could have been mugged or anything. We'd better be more careful or we'll get into serious trouble."

This time we walk straight across the border and into the Tanzanian Border Office. Our helper leaves us at the gate to the compound, pointing to the building we need to go to in order to get our entry visas. We are the only ones from our bus in the queue, which moves quickly. Our visas, which we bought in London before we left, are perfectly in order.

We wander outside to wait for the others and it's a few minutes before the bus pulls up and everyone troops off for their entry stamps. Everyone else has ridden across the border, having re-boarded the bus on the Kenyan side and waited to drive across.

As we sit and wait for the rest of the bus, Jen and I muse over our narrow escape at the hands of the border baddies.

"You don't think the notes are forgeries, do you?" she asks.

"Nah, they looked real to me", I reply, a hollowness opening up in my belly.

I open my wallet and pull out the two notes.

"Nope, genuine", I say.

I pull out another $100 bill just to make sure. It feels different, but then lots of dollar bills are different. I put the notes together and they are a slightly different size.

"Bugger", I say.

"Idiots."

"How stupid are we?"

Jen looks very annoyed, too annoyed to speak.

"Well, it's only £60 each", I say, trying to look on the bright side. "A lesson in how not to be conned could have been a lot more costly."

Jen is still speechless.

"What idiots though."

"I don't want to think about it", says Jen, fuming. "I don't want to tell anyone."

We continue in this vein, more quietly as others return from the border control and re-board the bus. We sit back on the bus ourselves. I continue to make light of it while Jen struggles to come to terms with how stupid we were. "We'd have been a lot more pissed off if we'd lost our cameras", I say.

"If this had been any of my previous boyfriends the holiday might as well have ended right here", she says. "I'm so annoyed. Are you not even a bit annoyed?"

"I'm very annoyed", I reply, "but there's nothing we can do about it now so we might as well forget about it and put it down to experience." If only I felt as rational as I sounded.

The rest of the journey leaves us both lost in thought. I bury my head in a book to forget about it. Jen attempts to sleep, although the look on her face indicates she's still troubled by the whole episode.

When we arrive in Arusha a number of people leave the bus. We wait on board as we are continuing on to Moshi. We are shooed off.

"This bus stops here", says the driver.

There follows a typical African scene. Much confusion (ours, our fellow passengers, the driver), many bystanders (other passengers, hotel staff, five seemingly un-connected men who have nothing better to do), plenty of items (our luggage), lots of raised voices (the driver, the staff, other passengers). In the midst of the hubbub another shuttle arrives. More confusion, more bystanders, more items and more raised voices eventually lead to us boarding the new shuttle with the Portuguese, a lone Western girl, two oriental girls, a young couple and a nun. All of our bags are piled on the back seat instead of the roof.

It's around 2.30pm when we leave. It's already mid-afternoon, yet there is still plenty of time to make Moshi and the football.

As stated in Andy's guidebook, the journey to Moshi takes 2

hours and we arrive in the town at 4.30, starving hungry and with ninety minutes to spare before kick-off.

Moshi houses some 150,000 people and is, according to the Tanzania Tourist Board, the coffee producing centre of the country. There are also sugar plantations, no doubt to make the granules to be added to the cups of coffee. Seasonal coffee auctions and a tour of the coffee-roasting factory are apparently the sights the passing visitor should not miss. Almost as an afterthought, they mention that there's a mountain you can climb too.

While the Tanzania Tourist Board gives a fair airing to each of the local attractions, all Western descriptions of Moshi are much more straightforward. You're in town for one of two reasons – because you are about to climb Kilimanjaro or because you have just climbed Kilimanjaro. The mountain should dominate the town's skyline, yet so far the main feature dominating the town is the plethora of adverts for Coca-Cola. Even the town clock tower is sponsored on all sides by the drink. Hopefully the mountain, which worryingly has a route up it called "The Coca-Cola Route", is less commercial.

Today's cloud-cover is preventing us from seeing Kili. Moshi is the Swahili word for smoke and I wonder if that's more a reference to cloud cover than a literal interpretation. Hopefully it's just cloudy down here and bright sunshine on the mountain side.

We pull up alongside the Impala Shuttle office. Our itinerary says that we'll be dropped off at the Keys Hotel, which the boys' map (how organised are they?) shows to be less than half a mile away.

"We could walk from here", says Andy, turning the map around and around to get his bearings right.

"We could", I say, hesitantly. I'm reluctant to volunteer us to walk anywhere with a rucksack before we need to. Half a mile with all our rucksacks is not going to help either of us make it to the top. Jen also has a shoulder injury from whiplash sustained in a car crash many years ago that sometimes lays her low for a whole weekend. Even though she never lets it stop her doing anything, it's not worth aggravating before we've even seen the mountain.

"Let's see if they drop us at the hotel", says Jen.

A few passengers leave the bus. A western girl is met by her boyfriend who, judging by their mutual fondling, she clearly hasn't seen for quite a while. One of the Portuguese women runs off to find a toilet. The rest of us stay on the bus. Two Chinese girls climb off and wait on the pavement for their bags. The driver climbs onto the roof to throw off the luggage. The two Chinese girls shake their heads at every bag he is about to drop on them. The Impala Shuttle office has a mirrored window, so from my seat I can see both the reflection of the driver on the roof and the two girls next to my open window of the bus.

"Black", shouts one of the girls.

The driver picks up a dark green bag and moves to throw it down.

"Black!" she shouts again. "A rucksack."

The driver stops mid-throw, looking annoyed that they don't want the dark green bag. He puts it to one side and picks up a black hold-all. He's about to throw it down when the girl shouts "No, a rucksack!"

"It's just down the road we're on, turn right at the next junction", says Andy.

I'm keeping an eye on the proceedings outside, making sure that the girls don't begin to share the driver's frustration and just settle for my rucksack instead of waiting for their own.

John nods slowly, as if weighing it up.

"No, a plain black rucksack", says the girl. Credit to the driver this time. The rucksack is indeed black but unfortunately has a red trim on the straps.

"Let's give it a couple more minutes", says Jen.

Andy turns the map again and then looks along the road as if trying to see the hotel.

"Is everyone up for trying to get some food before the game?" I ask. "I reckon we'll have time, and I'd rather eat earlier rather than later tonight."

Everyone agrees.

A black rucksack drops past the window. The girl drags it away from the bus.

"Red", shouts the other Chinese girl. I can see the driver with the dark green rucksack in his hands, leaning over the side of the bus roof.

The Portuguese leader gets off the bus and walks over to talk to the Impala Shuttle Office Manager. The Office Manager is standing watching the driver unload the bus. He has four men helping him watch.

Eventually all the passengers who have left the bus appear to have their luggage and are moving off. It's 4.40. The toilet-stopper returns and the nun climbs back on the bus clutching her bag. The Office Manager interrupts the Portuguese leader to bark instructions in Swahili to the driver. The driver looks at us all, then the nun, and then nods. He walks back to the bus while the Office Manager takes the Portuguese leader into the office.

The driver closes the bus doors and pulls away. Behind us the Portuguese leader runs back out of the office and waves at the bus. The Portuguese in the bus all look at each other, giggle, and mutter together in Portuguese.

We drive in the direction of our hotel, which is great given that Andy's map shows that it is close and there are still four groups of people on board that could need dropping off at four different hotels. We must be one of the first to be dropped off. We don't actually know if everyone is staying at the same hotel or if everyone is in our group or not. We could ask but we're not only British but British in the presence of other British. I'm guessing the nun isn't heading up the mountain – she looks about 70 – but I'm not discounting it. Faith is a wonderful thing, I'm told.

The bus takes a left, climbs a hill and stops outside a convent. The nun leaves, solving that short-lived mystery in an instant.

It's 4.50.

"The Keys is left at the corner", says Andy, moments before the bus reaches the corner and turns right to head back towards the Impala Shuttle Office. An edginess enters the bus and sits on the English.

The Portuguese leader gets back on to mocking cheers from his countrymen and women. We carry on back into town.

"Wasn't our hotel back the other way", I ask.

"Yes", says Andy, "we're heading back into town again now."

"Ah."

4.55.

We stop outside a hotel. Everyone almost certainly shares the same thought: I hope that's not our hotel. It is on a busy street, above a launderette and with the paint falling off the walls. There are shops on both sides and shabby pavement stalls in front. The bus driver says the name and the Portuguese slowly rise from their seats, looking at each other in disbelief.

The rest of us sigh and relax.

It's five o'clock.

There are just six of us left now. The next hotel is further out of town and inside a locked compound. It is tiny, no larger than a semi-detached house in suburban London. It is a million times nicer than the previous hotel but the one similarity is that it doesn't look like it has a bar showing the football. If we have to check in and then find a bar too we're almost out of time.

The driver says the name and the remaining two people leave the bus. The driver looks perplexed.

"Hotel?" he barks, in broken English.

"The Keys Hotel", replies Andy, in broken English.

"Two Keys Hotels", says the driver. "Which?"

Andy shows him the map.

"Ah", he shouts, annoyed that we've already been to that side of town. He gets back in the bus and we head off at twice the speed as before. Maybe he wants to see the game too.

We bounce past the Impala Shuttle Office for the last time, take the turn that Andy pointed out on his map 30 minutes ago and pull into the Keys Hotel. It's 5.10 and everyone is more worried about kick-off than the hotel which is, in fact, a pretty good hotel. Slightly out of town, it immediately has an advantage over the other places we've stopped in that, at the very least, it looks like a hotel. There is a reception, a restaurant and, most importantly, a bar with a TV screen.

Sitting on a cluster of easy chairs outside the front of the hotel, a group of about 10 people are having an introductory talk from their guides. They look happy and relaxed; maybe we should chill out a little too?

We check in at the front desk and are greeted by Limu, who introduces himself as our guide for the climb. He would like to give us an introductory talk. It's 5.15. We are all doing the same calculation in our heads.

"It will take 10, maybe 15 minutes", says Limu, unaware of the urgency.

We agree to drop our bags in our rooms and see him in 5 minutes on the chairs at the front of the hotel.

There is a large, 4m by 6m painting on the wall of the stairs. A snow-topped Kilimanjaro is in the background, overlooking a scrubby African plain where giraffes are roaming amongst sparse trees. The painting is semi-cartoon in style and the giraffes appear to be smirking at us.

It's 5.20.

Andy and John are already sat outside when we get back down. Limu is nowhere to be seen. We still barely know the boys, so we fill a few minutes finding out the polite basics of where they are from and what they do.

John works for a mobile phone consultancy, designing the software that makes all the gadgets on the phones work with the phone itself. He lives in Clapham South, London, and has a girlfriend of some short-term standing (and who became an ex-girlfriend not long after he returned to the UK). He supports Leeds United despite being originally from the Lake District.

Andy lives in Leeds, where he grew up and where he now works as an IT project manager for a large bank. He lives with his parents and doesn't have a girlfriend. He's a lot less geeky in real life than this two-sentence description makes him appear. He and John met at university and have been sharing an annual long holiday in each of the three years since they left. Last year they were in China and the year before that in Peru. All the holidays are of the backpacking outdoor variety, which is no surprise since they look like backpacking outdoor types – tall, slim and slightly rugged.

Although at this moment we are all a little concerned about our chances of seeing the game, John and Andy both appear to be laid back and amiable individuals. Both speak with gentle northern accents softened by time away from their area of origin. First impressions over the day indicate that John is the more outgoing and jovial of the two, Andy more straight and reserved.

It's 5.30.

There is tension in the air. There is only half an hour to kick-off and Limu has failed to appear. The conversation dries up as the minutes tick by. We agree that we are ravenous. We also agree that we'll eat after the game rather than before. A bird the size of a small boy lands on the highest branch of the tree by the gates to the hotel. The branch looks far too flimsy to carry the weight of the enormous creature. The bird appears unconcerned. It looks like a very fat vulture. Maybe it can sense there will be a kill soon if the guide takes any longer to arrive. Staring at the bird fills a few anxious seconds. We fill some more time by trying to guess where the mountain is. The overcast day has turned into an overcast evening with no sign of the cloud cover shifting. I imagine that I can see something through the clouds to the right of the hotel. Andy reckons that, according to his reading of the maps, the mountain should be more to the left. We all stare in one direction, then the other. There is no magical clearing of clouds to prove either of us right.

It's 5.40.

Maybe because I'm more impatient, maybe because the pre-match tension is not impairing my brain function quite as much, or maybe I just thought of it first – a simple thought springs to mind.

"Why don't I go and ask at reception and see if they know where he's gone?" I ask.

The receptionist hasn't seen him and suggests that I try outside the bar near the pool. Ah, the bar. Why didn't we think of that earlier? I wander through the restaurant and into the back of the bar. There are around 30 people in the bar, all occupying the best seats in front of the football. There are two screens. One is tiny, high on the wall in the corner and must be the usual method of watching the games or playing MTV. The other is clearly new for the world cup. There is a projector on a table in the middle of the room with a cable running through the chairs to a plug socket on the other side of the room. An image of the pre-match build-up is projected onto a bed sheet hung on the wall next to the smaller television. The room is dark so the picture shows up well. The bar counter is to one side of the screen; the main door to the bar is on the other. The projector, trailing cable and drinking fans are in the middle of the darkened room. The phrase "it has disaster written all over it" was coined for such a set-up.

I look out of the side door into the pool area and sure enough, Limu is sitting by the pool with a bottle of beer.

"Hello", he smiles.

"Hello", I say back. "Are you ready to give us the talk?"

"Yes, come and take a seat."

"I'll just get the others".

I walk back through the bar, carefully avoid causing the predicted disaster and head out of the front door to call the others over. They waste no time and thankfully head into the hotel and through the restaurant, avoiding the danger zone.

It's 5.45. Limu said the talk would take 10 or 15 minutes. We can still make kick-off.

We are the only people sitting outside the bar next to the pool. Inside, the players are on the pitch.

As soon as Limu starts to speak, it's very clear that kick-off is something we will hear and not see. He speaks very slowly, picking each word with what appears to be great thought. He repeats the important words two or three times, looking at each of us to make sure that we understood the significance of what was said. His native language is Swahili so he is probably working hard to converse in English.

We find out that we are the only four in our group, confirming Jen's fear that she will be the only girl with a bunch of blokes. Limu will be our guide and he will be helped by Patrick, who we will meet in the morning. Limu tells us the route we are taking and a rough plan for the next two days.

"We are taking the Umbwe Route. The Umbwe Route. The Whiskey Route. Whiskey. The hardest route. You have chosen this route … the hardest route … because you want … a challenge! You will be heroes. Heroes."

We all look at each other and shrug. No, that's not why we chose the route. We chose it because that's the route our tour company offered us. Actually that's not strictly true. It turns out that we all wanted to avoid the most popular Marangu, or "Coca-Cola" route, so named because it's the most popular, and happened to choose a company that offered this as the alternative. Now we're here and can see the extensive Coke advertising, it wouldn't surprise me to learn that Coca-Cola themselves had a hand in the choice of nick-name.

"I think it's going to be difficult enough without trying to make it harder", laughs Jen at Limu's mis-placed expectations.

"The Umbwe Route is the most beautiful route. The route for heroes."

He says he will explain the route further as we progress up the mountain. There are sighs of relief all round.

"Polè polè", he says. "The secret is polè polè."

We've all read about this in the guide books. In fact, whenever you mention that you are going up Kilimanjaro to anyone who vaguely knows anything about it, they all say these two words. "Polè polè", Swahili for "slowly slowly". Although it may seem palpably obvious that you won't be setting any sprint records as you struggle and strain to walk up a 5895m mountain, the trick is to walk even slower than you feel able to. This is especially the case at the start of the walk, when altitude doesn't feel like it is a problem. Foolhardy, fit and keen-as-mustard types who scamper along over the first couple of days suddenly hit a wall of tiredness and fail to reach the summit. The wiser and slower, who have taken their time early on to admire the scenery can carry on and summit without a care. It seems like an African version of the hare and the tortoise. Maybe the first climbers had a copy of Aesop's Fables and it struck a chord.

Scientifically, an explanation of why one person and not another is affected by altitude sickness is harder to find. Clearly most Westerners (and apart from the guides and porters, most climbers are Westerners) don't spend their average day walking 6 hours uphill at altitude, so the number of calories being burned by the average walker is going to exceed the 2500 average daily amount that we read on our packets of cornflakes. Maybe the speedier walkers simply don't stop enough to eat and the accumulated depletion of energy stores takes its toll after a few days, right at the time when things get really tough. Yet the simple solution to this would be to make sure you eat as much as you can, so as an explanation it is somewhat unsatisfactory.

Delving deeper, you begin to realise that many people don't want a scientific explanation for why polè polè works or why altitude sickness seemingly affects people at random. The mythology is far more compelling when it defies the collective understanding of modern science. That the short, fat, 70-year-old who trained by eating a few less biscuits a day has as much a chance of reaching the summit as the über-fit alpine-trained ironman-triathlete is part of the allure of the mountain. It's one of the reasons that I've managed to convince Jen to be sitting here right now. (Not, in the interests of clarity and for the avoidance of any risk to our relationship, that she is short, fat or anything approaching 70 years old, nor that I'm über-fit, alpine-trained or an ironman triathlete.) That we both have an equal chance of reaching the top is much more fun than the predictable boy-beats-girl scenario.

Although Limu's explanation is taking what feels like a very long time, he is imparting very little information and a delicate balance emerges during the conversation. There are things that we need to know and need to know tonight but I can see that everyone is reluctant to ask. The game has kicked-off. Even the simplest of questions results in a drawn out conversation.

"What time do we leave in the morning?" asks Andy.

"What time do we leave?" repeats Limu back at him.

"Yes, what time do we leave?" repeats Andy with barely a hint of impatience.

Limu ponders. "We leave ... we leave the hotel ... at 9 o'clock. 9 o'clock." He pauses before continuing. "We will drive for 2 ... maybe 3 ... 2 ... 2½ hours to the Umbwe Gate. The Umbwe Gate."

"OK, 9 o'clock", says Andy, keen to end that question.

"We are taking the Umbwe Route," continues Limu.

A look of panic flickers across Jen's face as she suspects that Limu is about to explain the route again. Fortunately he changes tack.

"You will have your bags ready at 8.30. 8.30. You know what equipment you need for the mountain", he says. It is not a question.

Silence. We've already discussed between the four of us that we are expecting to be told the kit-list to take with us. The tour company only sent us a list when we asked for it and the boys don't have one at all. Jen and I were still pondering whether we'll need our down jackets for the summit night, how much food to take and whether it will be shorts or trousers on the lower slopes. We still haven't even seen the mountain and our guide seems to be saying we know better than he does about what we need to take with us.

Jen, who has been the most keen to see the football and has been listening to the commentary as much as to Limu, is suddenly back in the room.

"Do you think you could give us a few pointers as to what we will need?" she asks.

Limu looks puzzled. Jen falters, seeing the first half disappearing before her eyes.

"Um, can you tell us what kit we have to take?"

We manage to keep Limu focussed on the essentials. The boys don't have poles, which they don't want and which Limu thinks are necessities. They reluctantly agree to hire a pair each and mutter to each other that they'll probably carry them rather than use them. Only Jen has gaiters. We boys – real men – don't mind a bit of mud on our trousers! It turns out that the mud isn't the problem, it's the scree on the descent that will fill our boots without them. We hire a pair each.

We don't resolve the down jacket dilemma. The boys don't have them, Limu thinks they are a good idea if we do have them but it's ok if we don't. Jen and I agree to pack them and see how cold it is. We appear to have everything else we can think of: two pairs of gloves and two pairs of thick socks for summiting, waterproof jacket and trousers for tomorrow. We finish the kit conversation with more hope than certainty that we are suitably equipped.

With what appears to be the end of the conversation, we shake Limu's hand, agree to meet at 8.30am with our bags and, as politely as we can, rush to the bar to watch the rest of the game.

Amazingly, the game is only 15 minutes old. It's still 0-0. The whole introduction has taken just 30 minutes. I have a momentary pang of guilt that maybe we were not as well-mannered towards Limu as we should have been before a more substantial pang of hunger swallows the pang of guilt. Aside from a muesli bar I haven't eaten for over 10 hours, and on a day when carb-loading is the recommended diet.

The score stays 0-0 until half time, when we decide that enough is enough on the lack-of-food front and head for the restaurant. We choose a table next to the windows overlooking the bar, so we can eat and watch the game on the big screen at the same time. Only two other people are in the restaurant, a couple from Canada who are paying not the slightest bit of attention to the game.

We order four plates of carbohydrates ("Spaghetti From age" for me) and four bottles of Kilimanjaro lager. They arrive as the second half kicks off. We chink a cheers and wish each other good luck, whether for the football or the climb to come isn't clear.

The second half is more tense than the first, for the English at least. Beckham is substituted, much to Jen's annoyance. My relative calmness about the match is spotted by Andy, so I explain that I'm Welsh. The next question always follows.

"So are you supporting England or Portugal?" asks Andy.

Having lived in England for half my life and having an English family on my mother's side, I have no difficulty in saying that I hope England beat Portugal. It's just that I can't be as passionate about it as they are.

"If Wales were playing Portugal in the World Cup ...", I begin.

"Unlikely", says Jen.

"… then you'd probably want Wales to win but you'd not be that bothered about the outcome."

There are nods all round. Suddenly the lights go out. It's barely 10 minutes into the second half and there's a power cut. A big groan fills the bar and disbelief spreads around our table. The waitresses hurry over with some candles for us. This is obviously a regular occurrence. We ask them how long the lights will be out for. They shrug and giggle, aware of the significance but, like me, somewhat detached from the panic around them. Jen has already texted home to get one of her housemates to text back any significant developments. She gets a text straight back, saying that Beckham is crying and looks even hotter than he usually does.

The lights come back on after 5 minutes. The little screen in the corner of the bar flickers on but the bed sheet is blank. It takes another few minutes for the barman to work out how to reset the projector. The bed sheet is filled by an image of Wayne Rooney making an awkward challenge. Oh dear, he's been sent off. There is a mixture of outrage and indignation from the table. The Portuguese do seem to be making a meal out of every challenge. Ronaldo rolls three times after a challenge from Lampard to prove the point.

The lights go out again, but only for a few seconds this time. It still takes a while to reset the projector although we can see enough of the small screen to know it's still 0-0. In this vein of power cuts and much ado about not very much the second half progresses to its goal-less conclusion. Extra time follows the same pattern. We finish the food and don't want to order any more beers so we pay the bill while waiting for the penalties. We all have a sense of an impending loss – can anyone remember England doing well at penalties?

Portugal score (1-0) – silence, heads in hands.

England miss (1-0) – "Good save?" I offer.

Portugal miss (1-0) – "Yay!" shouts Jen.

England score (1-1) – "Yes!" we all shout.

Portugal miss (1-1) – "Come on, we can do it!"

England miss (1-1) – "Poor Gerrard", says Jen.

Portugal score (2-1) – "Come on England!" shouts Andy.

England miss (2-1) – "Nooooooooo", says Jen.

Portugal score (3-1). Game over.

We head straight to bed. As I walk up the stairs the giraffes on the wall look even more amused than they did earlier.

"Look on the bright side", I say as I put the key in the lock. "We won't be worried about missing the semi-final now."

John and Andy close their bedroom door without saying a word. Jen looks at me in disbelief.

I continue digging a hole for myself. "If we were in London tomorrow", I say, "everyone would be really miserable. At least we've got our first day on Kili to look forward to."

Jen closes our bedroom door.

THE FIRST DAY OF THE CLIMB

Everest aside, Kilimanjaro is probably the most famous high mountain in the world. For example, can you name any of the other highest mountains on each of the seven continents? For the record and in order of height, they are Everest (Nepal, Asia, 8848m), Aconcagua (Argentina, South America, 6962m), Mount McKinley (United States, North America, 6194m), Kilimanjaro (Tanzania, Africa, 5895m), Elbrus (Russia, Europe, 5642m), Vinson Massif (Antarctica, 4892m) and either Carstensz Pyramid (New Guinea, Australasia, 4884m) or Kosciuszko (Australia, Australasia, 2228m), depending on which books you read. I was surprised to find that the one I thought I could name, Mont Blanc (France, Europe, 4808m), is largely disregarded as a highest peak thanks to a plate-tectonical interpretation of the location of the Caucasus and the watershed between Europe and Asia. For peak-baggers (people who climb as many mountains as they can in order to say they've climbed many mountains) it is deemed somewhat irrelevant – if you have climbed the seven summits then you are most likely to have climbed Mont Blanc anyway. For the rest of us they are all mountains that we've probably never heard of and almost certainly will never climb.

Phew, this is the big day. This is when we have the first chance to find out what all the fuss is about. We set the alarm early as we have to sort our belongings into three piles each: our main rucksack with everything we need for the whole climb, except for the bits we'll need during each day which we put into our daysacks, and finally a black bin bag to leave in the hotel with anything else we've brought along and don't need for the climb.

Now I'm a big fan of travelling light. Whereas most people will pack a rather large number of items just in case they'll need them, I'll tend to leave a rather larger number of items at home just in case I don't. There are few places in the world where you can't survive with just a passport, a credit card and the clothes you stand up in. And yet here I stand, in the midst of mountains of non-essential items of Alpine proportions. How did it happen, I'm asking myself with some despair.

Baden Powell has a lot to answer for with his simple motto of "be prepared". If you're a boy scout in the south of England then you have a fair idea of what to be prepared for. Rain? Bring a raincoat. Cold? An extra jumper will do the trick. Finding your way? Well, a compass and a bit of perseverance will probably bring you to a busy dual carriageway before you die of starvation (Kendall Mint Cake) or hypothermia (you did remember the jumper, didn't you?).

If you're a softy Londoner in the heart of Africa and about to climb nearly 4 miles into the sky then you haven't got a clue what to expect. "Be prepared" quickly translates into "Don't be under-prepared" which is as good as accepting that what you are really saying is "Be over-prepared". Hence my bedroom Alps. The internet is a good source of lists of what to take up Kilimanjaro, and a good way to be over-prepared is to download all the lists, combine them into a single master-list and take everything. Which is not far off what seems to have happened.

The down jacket is a good example. The internet lists vary between recommending it as an essential item for the summit attempt and suggesting that you can just as easily get by with a good fleece and thermals. Clearly what you don't want to do is arrive at the base and be turned away by a guide who is incredulous that you don't have one. Or even worse, you don't make it to the top because the weather takes a turn for the worse and it's down jackets or down the mountain. Then again, the mighty credit card can probably save the day if you find out near civilisation before the start of the climb.

Jenny contacted our tour company for a definitive answer but without much success. They checked their team and one of the girls had a friend who'd been up Kilimanjaro and had taken a down jacket. Did she actually need it though, pressed Jenny. Well, she wasn't sure but it was pretty cold on the summit night, came the answer.

Down jackets are not cheap. Between us we had already bought two four-season sleeping bags, a pair of walking boots and a water-proof jacket specifically for the trip, not to mention numerous sundry items such as roll-mats, thermals, wicking t-shirts, lip sun-block and all manner of remedies and potions to counter all ailments. Whether or not to spend another few hundred pounds on a pair of jackets that were unlikely to get worn anywhere ever again (unless we manage to save up the £10,000 required for an Antarctica trip) was a real dilemma. Down jackets are bulky too, especially at the cheaper end of the market. Avoiding carrying one has a definite packing advantage that just adds to the dilemma.

The dilemma would almost certainly have been decided on cost grounds had another answer not presented itself. Jen's dad owned a lemon-coloured one from a trip to Vienna (maybe lemon was a fashionable colour in Austria at the time?) and her mum's friend Sally owns a navy blue one from a trip to Nepal. They both kindly offered to lend them to us. How could we refuse? (We have already agreed that I will wear Sally's and Jen her dad's.) And now that we've brought them this far, it seems silly to leave them here in the hotel.

The weight limit on the rucksack that the porters will carry for each of us up the mountain is 12Kg. The down jacket goes into this rucksack, along with the other absolute essentials of a four-season sleeping bag, a roll-mat, two pairs of gloves, a warm hat, a scarf and a set of full-body thermals, towel, soap, contact lenses, toothbrush and toothpaste. The bags are already looking full and we've put both sleeping bags into my bigger rucksack to give Jenny any hope of fitting anything else into her smaller rucksack. Next are the must-haves-but-how-many, which include socks, boxer shorts, t-shirts, fleeces and trousers. The "how many" question is really a measure of how anti-social you can bear to be. We both opt for "not very". Then there are the could-do-withouts, which include spare water bottles, snacks, spare suncream and various toiletries. Some snacks go into my bag. Finally there are the why-did-I-ever-think-I'd-need-thats, which include shorts (it's still grey, overcast and cold outside) and binoculars. Both go into the bin bag to be left at the hotel. The bags look full and mine will certainly test the 12Kg limit.

Next is the daypack. No weight-limit here, just what we feel we can carry for the next 6 days. Absolute essentials – sunhat, water-bottle, fleece, raincoat, suncream, gaiters (or in my case space for the gaiters that Limu will bring), passport, important documents in a waterproof wallet, toilet paper, anti-malaria tablets. Must-haves-but-how-many – blister-plasters (1 packet, various sizes) in Jen's, spare water bottle (1x2litre) in mine. Could-do-withouts – snacks (I take the rest of them), spare socks (1 pair each), spare t-shirt (1 each), antiseptic hand-wash gel (1 bottle). Why-did-I-ever-think-I'd-need-that's – none. The bags are full but not too heavy.

Finally everything else goes into the black bin-bag to stay at the hotel. It's taken us about an hour to sort it all out. We hurry down to breakfast.

Jen and I continue to avoid dairy and fresh fruit and instead pile into the toast and jam. Andy and John join us mid-way through. We're all keen to get started and all a little apprehensive. The only other diners are a group of 6 people at a table at the far end of the room. They also look like they are about to climb the mountain. Jen is pleased that there are women in the group, none of whom look super-fit. No-one mentions the football.

The plan for the day is to be in reception with our bags ready at 8.30, set off from the hotel at 9 o'clock, take an hour's drive to the park gate and then walk for 6-8 hours to the first camp. The aim is to arrive at camp before dark, which falls at about 6pm.

We arrive in reception with our bags at 8.30. Split across 6 bags our belongings seem to take up twice as much space as before. The first step is to pay the local payment. Like many tours of this type, the cost of the holiday is split between an amount we paid in the UK before we left and a local payment (almost always in $US) paid on arrival. It's $1000 each and we are glad to no longer be carrying such a large amount of money around. Well, what we actually paid was $900 and a piece of paper that looks like a $100 bill each. Yes, I admit it. We passed on the forged notes. Now we're not proud of it and I've thought long and hard about whether or not to even mention it. We certainly talked through how we can possibly justify such an action and come up with many justifications. Here are the best three. First, for example, it will just go back into the economy so won't make any difference.

Second, we were given it here, so why shouldn't we pass it on here. Third, if we hadn't noticed the forged note, we would have passed it on oblivious to the fact any crime had taken place. And in response to the possible justifications, m'lud? First, such a large denomination most probably went straight to the bank, which would have spotted the forgery immediately. Who would then pay for the shortfall in cash? The hotel, which probably doesn't run at a great profit, or the receptionist who accepted the note, who probably doesn't earn that much all year? Second, as my mum was always at pains to point out, two wrongs do not, repeat do not make a right. Passing on our misfortune to someone else is hardly an act to be proud of. Third, well, yes, that might have been true, but for the fact that we actually did know about it. And if you know about it, then you also know it is the wrong thing to do.

So why did we do it? Why do something that you know is wrong when it costs you relatively so little to do something that is right? The only real mitigation is that it was a split-second decision. I hadn't expected to pay at that moment. The forged notes were still mixed with the real notes because we had tried hard not to think about what idiots we'd been. When I pulled out the money to pay, out came the forged notes with the real notes and they all got handed over. True, I could have said at any point "Oh, sorry, that's a fake note, take this real one instead". I just didn't. And then the moment passed and we were onto sorting out our bags and getting ready to climb Kili. Oh, and trying to blank out another crime from our minds.

After paying for the trip, the receptionist asks us what we would like to leave in the hotel safe. What a great idea, if only we'd known about it when packing our three piles of stuff. It's at this point that I realise that I can't find my wallet. (The irony is not lost on me.) I'd kept most of our cash in a money belt, using the wallet for small notes and credit cards. The wallet is no doubt buried within one of my three bags sitting on the floor of the reception and I'm loathe to tip them all out only to find it stuffed inside a sock at the bottom of the main bag. It's also not that critical for the next few days. I'm not planning on using it on the mountain, the few dollars we'll need to buy some snacks at the start of the trail are in my pocket already, and it hasn't actually got that much money in it anyway. Aside from around $US50, £UK50, our remaining 1000 or so Kenyan Schillings and my credit cards, the rest of our money is in my money belt. Given that finding it or not right now will make no difference, I decide to have a thorough search when we get back and hope it turns up in the meantime.

We check with Limu and he assures us that we won't need our passports, so we deposit our passports and money in the safe and head outside to join John and Andy at the bag weighing. Limu has arrived and is in charge out here. Porters quickly take our bags from us and hurry over to the scales, which are hung on a tree by the hotel gate. My main bag looks much bigger than everyone else's, which I'm sure is down to its construction until the scales tell a different story. 12Kg on the nail, according to the balance. Everybody else's bags are comfortably less than 10Kg. My daypack also looks larger than everyone else's. I'm not pleased to find I'm travelling with the heaviest load both physically and, thanks to our forged note incident, mentally.

Our transport to the park gate is a small mini-bus, about half the size of the shuttle from Nairobi. Our main bags are loaded on top while we sit and watch from inside. Patrick, our assistant guide, arrives with a quiet hello, a shy smile and a woman in a kitchen uniform carrying balls of aluminium foil containing our packed lunches. Last night I'd asked for a vegetarian version but a quick peek inside reveals that that seems to have been forgotten. I think the only thing I can eat is a hard-boiled egg (which is in my top three worst foods) and a kit-kat. I'm too embarrassed to point it out.

Suddenly Limu arrives from finishing the bag weighing.

"One vegetarian!" he says, "Who is the vegetarian?"

I raise my hand. "I think I've got a meat packed-lunch though."

"OK, OK", he says. A flurry of shouts of "vegetarian" is followed by the kitchen woman running off. We sit and wait.

The Canadian couple from the restaurant last night wander out of the hotel and over to our bus. Porters carrying their bags run over to the scales and Limu goes to oversee proceedings.

"Hi, I think we're joining you", says the man, smiling.

"Did you enjoy the soccer last night?" says the woman as she clambers into the bus and sits down with her back towards us.

And in those few seconds we have a complete glimpse of these two people and their relationship. He is a friendly, outgoing and warm person with a gentle, patient and curious nature. He is interested in finding out about us before climbing onto the bus. She is completely self-absorbed without a clue as to the effect she is having on those around her by her words and actions. Not only did she use that awful Americanism to refer to the beautiful game and ask if we'd *enjoyed* watching England lose in a World Cup quarter final, she also had no interest in finding out the answer. Still, I'm all for giving people a chance. First impressions are often wrong and, with another woman joining the group, it could work out well.

The kitchen woman returns with three more aluminium balls.

She gives the Canadians one each and then hands mine to me with the word "vegetarian". I take the ball, which looks and feels identical to the one I handed back. I'm pleasantly surprised to find a good selection of non-meaty items, albeit still with a hard-boiled egg.

"Hey, can I have vegetarian too?" asks the Canadian woman.

"You are vegetarian too?" asked Limu.

"Well, hey, no, not really, but I kinda just you know prefer it sometimes."

The kitchen woman runs off again and this time returns almost immediately with a new aluminium ball. The Canadian woman (who we have ascertained is called Abby) looks inside and grunts. The Canadian man (Bear – really, that's what he is called!) looks out of the window.

The trip to the park gate takes a couple of hours. The latter part is on dirt tracks through banana plantations, which is great fun. Small children run along after our bus, waving at us. We wave back, of course, to large grins. The main route to the park gate is blocked because the road is too muddy, so we turn back and take another even muddier road. The sky is still covered by heavy clouds. It looks like it will rain although we're pleased to have had none yet.

Our time at the park gate is our first experience of real "Africa time". I had been warned about Africa time a few years ago, when considering taking some time out to help an orphanage in Zimbabwe. A friend of mine runs a UK charity to support the orphanage and we had been discussing ways to help them. One suggestion was for me to go over and help out for a while. I pointed out that I had no practical skills to offer. She pointed out back that enthusiasm and organisation were skills enough. We traded points until we reached a real sticking point: how long to go for. I suggested a few weeks. She laughed and said I would just about get there and say hello before it was time to come back. "They work on Africa time. Things take as long as they take … and then a bit longer."

We arrive at Umbwe gate at 11 o'clock and jump out of the bus, keen to be on our way. If it takes us 7 hours to get to the first camp, we need to be on our way very soon if we are to arrive before dark. Around us there is no sense of urgency, only a lot of faffing. We have 15 porters to carry all our bags, tents and food. Most of them are milling around while two of them weigh our bags again.

The park gate is not a gate but a small, 150m square clearing in the forest at the side of the mud track. The trees are tall, some 20-30m high all around us and a deep, dark green in colour. There is a wooden building at the far side, an open-sided hut not unlike a pagoda in the centre, another smaller one to the left and a row of toilets to the right. We are told to wait in the central hut while our bags and the rest of our necessities are carried to the hut on the left. I need the toilet and wander over to choose between "men", "women" and "porters". Given the state of the hole in the ground for men, I cannot imagine what hides behind the door marked "porters". I hope the door marked "women" leads to a lavatorial nirvana. Jen assures me it doesn't.

Africa time drifts along and we do our best to fill the time with our own faffing. We put on our waterproof trousers, check the length of our walking sticks (which are of the extendable telescopic variety), put on our gaiters, re-tie our laces, take our photos next to the "Umbwe Gate" sign at the start of the trail and muse over whether it will rain or not. Jen and I are caught out by the lack of snacks available for sale. Last year on the Inca trail I couldn't move for women and children selling snickers and cagoules, to the extent that we struggled to even get off the bus at the start of the walk. I had confidently assured Jen that it would be just the same here, yet there is not a sweet-seller or cagoule-trader in sight. We compare our meagre haul of fake Mars and grain bars with John and Andy's bursting bags of chocolate, nuts and raisins. If we're to follow the advice of "eat as much as you can to increase your chance of reaching the top", I'm in danger of having to eat the hard-boiled egg.

There are a surprising number of people standing around the clearing, just standing around and watching the proceedings. The proceedings involve a surprising number of people standing in the clearing, watching surprisingly few people actually doing something useful. The crowd of maybe 50 people includes men, women and children. It's Sunday lunchtime, so maybe this is the Tanzanian equivalent of watching The Politics Show or Songs of Praise. It's probably more fun and thankfully involves no politicians or hymns.

An hour later, the scene just described has barely changed. Some monkeys high in the trees behind the hut provide some excitement, especially for Bear. He runs to the edge of the clearing and calls to Abby to come and see.

"Honey my camera lens is stuck", she whines.

"Quick or you'll miss them."

"I told you my lens won't open hun!"

Honey Bear stays where he is, enthralled by the monkeys and ignoring Abby's whining. This winds her up even more. She turns to us and complains some more about her stuck lens and how it's been that way since they arrived. John offers to take a look.

"No, you know, it will come loose, it's just stuck, you know, it always happens at the worst time." She continues to pluck pathetically at the lens, sighing.

The monkeys are the first real wildlife we've seen on the trip and we too are excited to take a look. The monkeys are at the top of the tallest trees, some 30m up. The locals are amused by our excitement, and regard us in the same way that we regard tourists in London's St James Park getting excited over the squirrels. I wonder if zoos in Tanzania have squirrels in them the way we have monkeys. Maybe we give them squirrels and they send us monkeys? I remember the cage of mallard ducks I saw in Lima zoo and finding it quite funny. Maybe there's a whole world zoo trading economy out there?

A 4x4 pulls up and two men with two large books climb out. They come into the central hut and open their books. They are here to log our entry into the park and to give us our permits. They need our names, addresses and passport numbers.

We run off to find Limu, who is organising the piles of kit for the walk.

"We need our passports", I say to him.

"Yes", he says.

"When we asked you at the hotel, you said we could leave them in the hotel safe."

"No no, you need your passport numbers to sign in."

"Our passports are in the hotel."

Who knows how this apparent deadlock would have been resolved had I not remembered that I'd put a photocopy of our passports in the back of my rucksack. Most likely, I think we'd have made up the numbers, as the two permit men with their big books were not checking anything. I ask Limu where my rucksack is and he leads us to the bag weighing area. My bag is wrapped up with another inside a big thick plastic bag. We drag it out, I delve in and I find the copies of the passports without having to empty too much out of the bag. I repack the bag, help the porter re-stuff it into the larger plastic bag and quickly rejoin the others to sign in. As I enter my details I notice that the last people to enter the park through this gate came on Wednesday 28 June, 4 days previously.

Surely this must be all we've been waiting for, yet there is little indication that we are about to begin. Inactivity is bustling all around us when, suddenly, everything happens at once. Another bus pulls up, music playing loudly, and a group of middle-aged male South Africans step out into the clearing. A guide calls the Canadians and they head out of the clearing and onto the trail, quickly disappearing into the forest. There is an unspoken feeling of relief between the four of us that they have their own guide. Abby had the potential to be tougher going than the trail. A few minutes later, Limu calls over to our band of four heroes and, with much excitement and more than a little trepidation, we don our rucksacks and start the walk.

"Polè polè", says Limu, setting the pace right from the start.

"Polè polè", we all cheer back. Walking slowly feels awkward to begin with. Having waited so long to get going, to be finally on our way and then to have to hold back the enthusiasm is a little strange. It feels like driving a Ferrari in a 30-zone or maybe a little more accurately in my case, a Punto in a 20-zone.

The slight drizzle that had begun to fall as we waited in the clearing stops as soon as we start walking, leaving the sky covered in a thick heavy cloud and the air extremely humid. Limu explains that we are in a cloud forest and that the weather is often like this.

The trail is wide enough for two 4x4s to pass and the incline is gentle but constant. The ground is muddy and firm. We could be in Wales. Well, in the summer, at least.

We quiz Limu with a variety of questions. His English is a little stilted but very good. He is chattier today than yesterday evening. Or maybe we are the chattier ones.

Limu lives in Moshi with his wife. She has never climbed Kilimanjaro, and he seems amused at the thought of her doing so. They have one child, a one-year-old girl. Limu climbs the mountain about 12 times a year. Sometimes this can mean going straight back up the day after coming down, while at other times it can be 3 months between walks. He takes the work when he can get it.

A thin dark line crosses the path in front of us. It's a procession of safari ants 5 wide and 2 deep, clambering over and around each other as they cross our path. The line comes out of the forest on one side and disappears into the forest on the other, a seemingly endless trickle of black flowing through the trees. I straddle the line and bend down to take a picture. Limu warns me to be careful. A few years ago he was woken in the night by being bitten by about fifteen of the ants. The bites are very painful and can be fatal in large numbers. I step to one side of the line, take my picture and carry on up the trail.

We ask Limu how many times he has climbed Kilimanjaro. This is his 109th trip. Does he still enjoy it? He shrugs. It's a job; there are worse jobs and there are better jobs. Would he climb up the mountain if he wasn't guiding? Again a shrug. Maybe. I read this as the only polite and correct response that he can give us without actually lying. Would he really climb up the mountain again if he didn't have to? Not in a million years, but he can't tell that to us, the people who are paying him to take them to the top of a mountain he would never climb by choice.

We stop for lunch at around 2pm, having passed the Canadians a while earlier. Bear was already carrying Abby's daypack and Abby was already complaining of sore feet. The trail is steeper now and has narrowed to about one-vehicle wide. We all need the toilet, which is fine for the boys but not so fine for Jen. While the trail is flat and clear, the forest on each side is impenetrable. It leaves nowhere for a girl to squat down out of sight. We agree to look the other way and shout if a porter comes along.

The packed lunch is very good, albeit small compared to a normal lunch at home. I try and trade my boiled egg for something, anything, but nobody is interested. I can't even give it away. I'm still hungry, it's a long time until dinner and we don't have a surfeit of snacks. I take a deep breath and bite into the egg. Blimey it is just as bad as I remember. (I still shudder at the thought of it.) It has the texture of soggy textbooks, the smell of poo and the taste of, well, nothing really. I don't understand how people eat the little devils. Thankfully I've saved my kit-kat until last, which removes the unpleasantness out of my mouth.

The Canadians arrive as we are finishing our lunch.

"Do any of you have a plaster?" shouts Abby up the path. "I've got a blister."

Jen says she's got some blister plasters that Abby can have. Abby looks dubious, so Jen gets them out of her pack while Abby sits down and removes her socks. There's no sign of a blister or even any reddening of the skin, so the plasters go away and Abby sits on the tree-stump and rubs her feet. Bear gets out their packed lunches, which Abby refuses to eat.

"I can't eat that, I don't want that, that's washed in …"

"It's pretty good", I interrupt, trying not to think about the egg.

"It's too risky to eat any of the meat over here, and the vegetables are all washed in unclean water."

"The cheese sandwich is just cheese and bread", I suggest.

"I'll stick to my trail bars. Does anyone want my lunch?"

A few minutes ago I'd have grabbed it but the egg has finished off my appetite. We suggest that she gives it to one of the porters, so Bear does just that for her.

We leave the Canadians to their troubled lunch and the forest soon muffles the twanging accent. The vegetation is green and damp. Every leaf looks ready to drip a blob of water onto anything that passes by, yet I'm wet from sweat, not forest. The air changes from cloud above us to cloud around us. We've all left our waterproof jackets off since lunch and, even in the clouds, there's no need to put them back on. The forest turns quite eerie, with few sounds except for the rustling of Jen's and my waterproof trousers. There's no need to keep them on any more but it's too much hassle to take them off. The line of sweat down my bum crack can dry off later.

We talk to Limu about the mountain and the different routes up it. Of the 20-25,000 people who climb the mountain each year (a number that is doubling every 10 years), 85-90% walk the Marangu Route. No surprise it's known as the Coca-Cola Route and I now understand the lack of adequate chocolate supplies at the Umbwe Gate. If you are a local snack seller and 85% of your target market travels through one point, you set up your stall at that point. As the four of us wander through our own private idyll, it is hard to imagine that there is a route not so many miles away with maybe 100 people sharing the splendour. They will also sleep each night in communal huts rather than a tent. Again, it must be quite a different experience and more like a school trip than an adventure in the African wilderness.

Each route is named after the village near where it starts. While the Marangu Route attacks the mountain from the south east village of Marangu, the next most popular route comes in from the south west village of Machame. The Machame Route is a good route, says Limu, as it is away from the crowds of Marangu, much more beautiful and people have a better chance of reaching the top due to the extra night it takes.

After two or three days, the Machame Route joins the Shira and Lemosho Routes. These two routes, often interchangeably referred to as the Shira Route, form the western approach to the mountain. The Shira Route starts further north and crosses the Shira plateau. The Lemosho Route starts in the forest which, if our current surroundings are anything to go by, must be the more favourable way to begin.

There is a path encircling the mountain which all the routes either cross or follow a part of. While the North Circuit Path is little used and not part of any route to the summit, the South Circuit Path is a much more trodden and integral part of the ascent of Kilimanjaro. Not long after the three Machame, Limosho and Shira Routes join up, there is a choice of whether to head straight to the top via the difficult Arrow Glacier and Western Breach, or to take the more leisurely approach via the South Circuit Path. The former is now regarded as unsafe and not used, so trekkers usually circle south. After a further day's walk, they will reach the point where the Umbwe Route joins the South Circuit.

The Umbwe Route ascends from the south, starting between Marangu and Machame. Limu again enthuses about the Umbwe Route – the most difficult, the most beautiful, the most interesting, the least trodden, and so on. He probably says the same when he's guiding on the Marangu Route, although there is little around us to prove him wrong about Umbwe. It is also one of the shortest routes up the mountain, especially if you ascend via the closed Western Breach.

The final route is the most different of all, the Rongai Route. It is the only trail to approach the mountain from the North, starting near the border with Kenya, and there are chances of seeing elephants along the way. (Now why didn't we know that before we booked?) For the final ascent, the Rongai Route joins the Marangu Route in the climb up to Gilman's Point, where many people decide that enough is enough and head back. From there the path continues up and is joined for the final few yards to the summit by all the other routes that have travelled around the South Circuit Path.

There is one final route on the mountain, and it's a descent-only route. The Mweka Route is the most direct route from the summit and off the mountain and is used by those people who have climbed up from Machame, Lemoshu, Shira and Umbwe. Marangu and Rongai trekkers leave via Marangu, which again makes me think that anyone using the Marangu Route is seriously short-changed. Not only is it relatively crowded, you also have to walk back exactly the way you came. Maybe we won't care by that point.

The path has narrowed to barely a metre-wide and we suddenly step onto a recently improved section that would look at home in a nature reserve in the UK. There are logs down each side with a solid dirt trail in between. Every few metres a log crosses the path to hold it all in place. Even though the path is new, some of the logs are already rotting and they crumble when we stand on them. Limu says that, when he last walked up this path last year, the path was not like this. This is much better. With the apparent rate of erosion of some of these logs, the path won't be like this next year either.

Jen sees a stick insect on the path and we stop and take a look. She has a remarkable ability to see any wildlife that might be lurking around, no matter how well hidden. Maybe it's a finely-honed self-defence mechanism in case any spiders happen to be around (she can't even look at a picture of a spider without breaking into sweaty palpitations). It's great to have her around on any walk though. We walked across Richmond Park in the spring and she spotted the dear and a bat well before I did, a wren camouflaged against a tree that I struggled to spot even when staring straight at it and, the icing on the cake, a terrapin in the river. It might have been the size of a side plate but nobody else on the busy riverbank had spotted the very non-native reptile.

There appears to be more wildlife in Richmond Park than around us here in the forest. We can't hear any birds singing and there are no strange rustling noises. There are certainly no more monkeys, so the sight of the stick insect is cause enough for a break and a picture. It really is well camouflaged and only gives itself away when it moves. Limu waits patiently. Excitement over, we carry on up the trail.

The forest is very close on each side of us and the cloud hangs between the trees and around us on the path. Without noticing, I've settled into polè polè very easily. It turns out to be a very sociable speed to walk at. Nobody is racing ahead and getting frustrated at having to wait for the group to catch up. Neither is anyone trailing at the back, finally catching up only for the group to race away again before there's a moment to rest. Everyone can talk as no-one is out of breath from walking too quickly. We're all rarely more than a few metres apart, bunching together as the path steepens and stretching apart as it levels off a little. Even the sometimes fraught question of who is at the front and back just resolves itself to be largely determined by toilet stops – whoever stops for a wee simply catches up at the back and polè polès along until the next person takes a leak and they move forward up the group.

The nature reserve path lasts for about half an hour before coming to an abrupt halt. Then it's down to single file and we're clinging to tree roots to haul ourselves up sometimes near-vertical scrambles. It's great fun and everyone enjoys it immensely. This is what the guidebooks had led us to expect and, rather than being a complete slog, it felt more like being a kid in a huge adventure playground.

"Hey", shouts John as he reaches the top of yet another scramble, "blue sky!"

We stop our climb and look up. Sure enough, the cloud is wispier and there is a tiny patch of blue sky straight up above us.

"Yay!"

Everyone is lifted by it, not that we weren't feeling pretty chipper anyway. It's the first bit of blue sky we've seen since we arrived in Africa two days ago and we've had to work for it. Either the cloud is clearing or we're climbing through it. The sun is trying to blast through over to the left but isn't quite making it just yet.

The path now leads us along a wooded ridge, just slightly below and to the left of the top of the ridge. The right hand slope of the ridge is almost sheer in parts, albeit still mainly covered in trees except for the absolutely vertical parts. The left hand slope is much gentler and is the normal dense forest we've been walking through all day. The cloud around us has cleared completely and the cloud above us is much brighter. Every now and then the path winds up to the top and edge of the ridge, and the drop away to the right is awesome. The cloud is really starting to shift and more and more blue sky pokes through. The views across the valley are opening up to show endless wooded valleys and ridges laced with clouds. It all looks soft and strokable, like cotton wool rolling along folds of green velvet.

I stand and stare for a bit, catching my breath and waiting for the others to catch up.

"It's Kili!", I shout, suddenly noticing that way above the clouds, way above the ridges and, most importantly, way above us is the un-mistakable, snow-covered peak of the mountain we are hoping to climb. If we were lifted by finally seeing some blue sky, we are even more excited by finally seeing Kilimanjaro.

"Awesome", says John, stopping next to me.

"That ... is ... amazing", says Andy.

"Wow", says Jen.

The peak looks such a long way away, both horizontally and vertically. After the gloom of the cloud forest that we've been walking through all day, the glimpse through the dark tree branches of the startlingly white mountain peak is like looking into another, more vibrant, world. The colours are unreal – bright white snow, powder blue sky, velvet green valleys – all framed by the deep, dark and damp forest branches that keep us within their grip. A porter walks past with a reed basket on his head and one of our rucksacks on his back. We move to one side to let him pass and he continues up the path. His arms hang rigidly by his side and his back is perfectly straight, no doubt to cope with the weight and awkwardness of his dual load. This might be one of the wondrous sights of the world to us. It is easy to forget that to most of the people on the mountain it's just the backdrop to their daily job.

All day we have marveled at the porters as they have steadily trudged past us, almost always with both a bag on their backs and a sack on their heads. When I walked the Inca trail, it was always when I was most exhausted and ready to take a break that a porter would spring swiftly past with a gas bottle or a dining table strapped to his back, apparently not even out of breath. At least in Peru there was a well-laid stone path for most of the trail. Here there is a muddy brown streak between close hugging trees. At intervals the branches reach out and grab at the sacks on the porters heads, forcing them to perform a contorted limbo dance. When we are clinging to tree roots, the porters doggedly stick to using just their legs. They have no sticks to steady themselves and rarely, if ever, use their hands, as to do so risks losing the sack on their heads.

The porters undoubtedly put our quest into context. Here are we Westerners, making out we are on an epic journey that few people will ever make, when there are people here regularly making the same journey with a kitchen stove on their back and a picnic table on their head. It is a humbling thought. I take solace in the fact that the porters only have to climb to 4600m, a good three-quarters of a vertical mile below our final destination. It makes me feel momentarily better about just carrying my small daypack, anyway. The moment disappears as another overloaded porter overtakes us.

There's another thing makes my personal quest appear a little less incredible. It is very clear how much extra effort Jen, at five feet three-quarters of an inch tall, needs to make compared to John, Andy and me at around 6 feet. To climb up some of the slopes, Jen needs to lift her knees almost to her ears in order to reach the next step, when in the same position a few seconds later I am well within a comfortable stretch. The difference at times is comical. Yet she is determined to not be the person who holds up the group in any way, and never once over the whole day has she complained or asked us to wait.

It is dusk as we arrive at the Umbwe Caves, our camp for the night and the first of 4 camps on our way to the top. The caves are little more than an overhanging rock next to a bog. Our camp is a 5-minute walk above the caves, where the ground is drier, and we arrive at around a quarter past six. The camp is at 2850m, some 1150m higher than Umbwe Gate where we started. We have climbed almost the height of Ben Nevis and we still have another three vertical kilometres to reach the top.

The camp is just another part of the mountainside forest with the underbrush cleared. A few tree stumps show that some of the larger trees have been removed but the ground is snaked with roots and dotted with rocks. Our tents have already been erected by the porters and our rucksacks are sitting inside them. Jen and my tent is on a gentle slope. I can see that much of the night is going to be spent crawling back to the top of the tent after we've slid down to the bottom again. We look over at John and Andy's tent. Only John's rucksack has arrived, much to Andy's concern. John is more concerned with the angle of their tent, which is at a similar angle to ours.

"It's going to get cosy tonight when I roll on top of you!" jokes John.

"It's not going to be cosy at all if my rucksack doesn't turn up", grumbles Andy.

John dives into the tent and shouts from inside.

"Awww, there's an enormous root right across the middle!"

I laugh and crawl into ours to check the ground. The tent is yellow and a good-sized, two-person dome with a porch. It's in reasonable condition. Apart from the slope there's just one sharp stone right in the middle, which I manage to tease out to the edge. There are a couple of roots at the edges that won't bother us. We've got Thermo-rests to put on top of the roll-mats that the porters have given us, so apart from the slope I think we'll do pretty well. I crawl out to see Andy's rucksack arrive. John has gone to find a toilet. Andy drags his bag into their tent.

Jen and I feel surprisingly good. No blisters, no aches, no exhaustion. Altitude sickness is not a problem yet as it mainly starts to affect people at 3000m and above. If we'd been suffering from it already then we'd be in serious trouble and not at all likely to make the summit.

John appears, climbing up the slope from behind their tent.

"That has to be the worst toilet I have ever used", he says.

"Noooo", says Jen.

"Is it really that bad?" I ask.

"Seriously, I won't be using that one again. There is shit all over the floor. Try another one."

"Hmmm, let's find one before it gets dark", I say to Jen.

There is enough daylight to see across the camp although it is fast fading. The sun has set around the side of the mountain and the trees are covering much of the sky, so it feels darker than it should at this time of day.

Jen and I dig out the head-torches and toilet paper from our bags and scurry off to find a toilet. Our tents are at the lowest edge of the camp and John had used the toilet on our side. There are more toilets across the camp, although there is no easy way around or through the camp. Even though the area has been cleared of undergrowth, no effort has been made in making paths around the trees, roots, rocks and slopes. We stumble along and come across the South Africans who arrived at the gate as we left at lunchtime. The last of their group is just arriving amidst some back-slapping and cheers. There is a toilet very close to their camp, poor guys. It's an open wooden hut without a door, the walls shaped like a number 6 so that you can't see straight in. The floor is wooden planking and the roof is held about a foot above the walls by the corner posts, no doubt to let all the nasty odours escape. Even from 20 metres away we can tell that the smells are escaping well.

We climb over another man-sized tree root towards it and one of the South African comes out of the toilet, zipping up his fly. He walks with the confidence of a man who has just climbed a mountain and found it wasn't too difficult after all. Or maybe he just walks with the confidence of a South African.

"I wouldn't go in there if I were you", he says, and walks off to join the others.

Maybe he was walking with the confidence of a man who has just had a man's poo.

"After you", I say to Jen.

"Thanks."

I wait outside the toilet. As the darkness falls the temperature is dropping quite sharply. It's not helped by the wet, sweaty clothes I'm still wearing.

"Well?" I ask a few minutes later as Jen emerges from the gloom. She wrinkles her nose.

I switch on my head-torch and enter the box of delights,

breathing through my mouth to avoid gagging at the stench. The toilet space is a metre square with a hole in the middle the size of a letterbox. Over the hole there is a plug of wood with sawn-off broom handle stuck into it. The floor is wet with urine that has not found its target and there are lumps of what thankfully looks like mud rather than shit all over it. The walls are also covered with what looks like mud of a similar colour. If it's not mud on the walls then someone has had a serious problem in here. I pull the wooden plug out of the hole, do my business, put the plug back and get out as fast as I can. Jen has already retreated to a safer distance and it's only when I feel a breeze on my face that I breathe through my nose again.

"Not as bad as I thought it would be", I say.

"I was more bothered about there being spiders in there", says Jen.

We clamber back to our tent, in the dark taking a completely different route to the one on the way. John and Andy are inside their tent. We sit on a tree stump and take off our boots. I hope the walk back from the toilet has wiped off any of the nastier elements they might have found in there. Our socks are damp and we hang them out to dry over a set of tree roots that jut jauntily out of the ground. Next it's the waterproof trousers, which are dry on the outside and wet with sweat on the inside. Nice. I've been wearing knee supports over both knees and they are also soaking wet. They smell too. I jam my walking sticks into the ground and balance a knee support on each of them. My t-shirt is the final wet piece of clothing to be draped over the tree roots. It has a thick white salt line delineating the extent of my sweatiness.

The evening is cooling and we are feeling it more now that we've taken off our wet clothes. Jen and I take our daypacks into the tent and zip-up the inner and outer doors. We change out of the rest of our clothes into some dry kit from our rucksacks and feel instantly warmer. We blow up our Thermo-rests, lay them on the roll-mats and unroll our four-season sleeping bags on top. It all looks pretty warm and cosy. There is plenty of space down the sides for our rucksacks and daypacks so they don't crowd the bed space.

We are just about to lay down and say "Phew, well done" when Limu calls us.

"Tea time!"

Limu told us on the walk that we would get hot drinks and biscuits when we arrived at camp followed by dinner a little later. Given the time and that it is getting dark, I'd assumed that we'd skip the hot drinks and head straight for dinner. In fact, I'd rather hoped that would be the case. Now we've stopped I'm feeling ready for bed, even though it's not even 7pm. I can't blame jet-lag either – in London it is only four in the afternoon.

We drag ourselves out of the tent. Our drying clothes are still damp and we throw them into the tent rather than leave them out all night. John and Andy are ahead of us walking down the hill towards the group of porters below.

John laughs. "This is unreal", he says, as he's ushered into a tent.

"Chuffin' 'eck", says Andy.

Jen and I follow them inside, where we can just about stand up.

"Wow", I laugh.

Inside there's a square dining table laid with a table cloth, napkins, cutlery and crockery. There are four chairs, one on each side of the table. The back of the tent has a window down the mountain, through which the last remnants of light are seeping in.

"I didn't see any of this go past us up the mountain!" says Jen

We slump into the chairs and a flask of hot water is brought out to us by our waiter. We ask his name but I can't make out his reply. I think his English is good but he is too shy to speak clearly in case he makes a mistake. He is a little overweight and looks about 50 years old. In addition to his waitering duties I have little doubt that he has carried a rucksack or two up the mountain, so must be feeling tired. I know I wouldn't want to wait on anyone right now.

We have a selection of coffee, tea and Milo on the table. It turns out that John and I share a rare foible – neither of us normally drinks hot drinks. My reason is sheer impatience at waiting for it to cool down. When I want a drink of something, I want to be able to drink it straight away and not wait the 5 or 10 minutes for it to cool down. If I ever do succumb to the temptation to buy a hot drink, I usually end up burning my tongue because I don't wait long enough. This only makes me less interested in having another hot drink, of course. The more hot drinks you drink, the hotter you can drink them. If you never drink hot drinks, your mouth doesn't build up a tolerance to the temperature and you have to wait longer to be able to drink them. It's a vicious circle and one I'm normally happy to drop out of altogether and just not drink hot drinks. (It has been pointed out that I could learn to be more patient but I don't have the time for that.) A by-product of not drinking hot drinks is not drinking caffeine. I don't have a great affinity for fizzy pop, including coke, so I very rarely have any caffeine in anything. Once again this means that I have no tolerance for it. If I drink a strong coffee or tea in the afternoon I will struggle to sleep that night.

These are exceptional circumstances, however. There is no alternative to boiled water and I'm cold. To avoid the caffeine, I have a choice of plain hot water or Milo. We've never heard of Milo. John dubiously picks up the tin to check the ingredients. He breaks into a grin.

"Milo, the food drink of future champions!" he reads. "That's good enough for heroes like us."

"Yay!" cheers Jen.

"Milo it is then", I agree.

"Four heaped spoons per mug", says John. "I hope they've got a few crates out there."

We all pass on the tea and coffee and take a few heaped spoonfuls of future champion powder with hot water. It's actually not bad, a chocolatey concoction full of calories, carbs and chemicals that warms the belly. The waiter comes back with a plate of biscuits and leaves again. We dunk in communal pleasure.

(I mentioned Milo to an Australian friend when I got back home and it turns out to be an Aussie staple, like Vegemite and Tim-Tams, that makes your average antipodean turn gooey-eyed and think of home. Apparently more Milo is sold each year than the weight of the Sydney Harbour Bridge. Perhaps this is the secret ingredient behind Australia's sporting success?)

The waiter returns to clear away our pots, so we leave the dining tent and walk back up the hill for a lie down before dinner. A pair of head-torches bobs its way through the camp beside us.

"Well done", says Jen. "You've made it! You can chill out with Milo and biscuits now."

"I'm going straight to bed", replies a familiar Canadian voice.

"Well done, anyway", I say.

There is no reply. The head-torches bob up into the darkness above and beyond our tent.

"I bet that was hard in the dark", says John.

"And when you're knackered at the end of the day as well", I agree.

"She should eat or she's really going to struggle", says Jen

"He seemed alright though", says Andy, referring to Bear. Bear had still been carrying Abby's bag as he walked silently past us. From what I could make out through the darkness he didn't looked too tired.

There is a silence for a few seconds while we consider what it would have been like had they been walking with us. We couldn't have left her behind and so we'd all have just been arriving. There is no contest between an annoying Canadian and a bellyful of warm Milo.

"Where was your loo?" asks Andy, pointing his head-torch at Jen.

"Sort of that way", waves Jen in the general direction of the toilet. "Turn right at the South Africans."

Jen and I lay down on our bed and chat through the last few hours. It's been a fantastic first day. We are both pleased to have made it without any real struggle. The path was muddy but not cloyingly so. The mountain was steep but not impassable. The pace was just right: fast enough to make it here before dark, slow enough so that nobody felt pressured to keep up. The boys are good fun, the group size is spot-on, the weather was ideal for walking, the view of the summit was amazing, even the hot drink finish was pretty good. It's so good to have a day behind us as well. Everything we'd read about the route turned out to be true, yet it was manageable and fun. We now have some confidence that the walking is going to be OK. There is just the small matter of the altitude to overcome next.

The hour until dinner passes quickly and I'm surprisingly hungry again when the waiter calls us. The table has been re-laid in the dining tent. Dinner is three courses, although it almost doesn't even start when the waiter can't remove the lid from the pan of mushroom soup. The hot air inside the pan has contracted in the cold as the waiter has carried it to us, so the soup is sucking the lid tightly onto the pan. The waiter eventually gives up and goes for help, so Andy has a go at breaking the seal by sliding a knife between the pan and lid. It doesn't budge. Limu and another porter return with the waiter. It's a team effort now; the waiter holds one side of the pan, the porter the other and Limu attacks the top with a knife and a grin.

"If we heat it up again the lid might release itself", I suggest.

Then there is a hiss and a rattle and the lid is off. We all clap and cheer and Limu takes a bow. The mushroom soup smells fabulous.

The starter is followed by rice and goo for main course and slices of mango for dessert. Everything is incredibly tasty and we devour the lot, finishing with a Milo each. There's no light in the tent other than our head-torches, and we're reluctant to use them too much only to find we are out of batteries when we try and reach the summit. Everyone agrees on an early night and, after toilet trips and teeth-brushing, we're in bed by 10pm.

The four-season sleeping bags are beautifully warm. Jen and I bought new four-season sleeping bags for the trip and found identical and opposite ones so that we can zip them together into one great mega-bag. (You need opposite zips or one person has the hood over their face.) When we tried them out in Jen's room back home, we could only stay in the bag for a couple of minutes before it became far too hot and I had to escape. I was a little worried the bags might be too warm but right now they are blissful. The bags are quite enormous and the space in the double bag is huge. During the practice at Jen's we both managed to both fit into one bag. (Well, you have to try these things.) Unfortunately it was a bit too much of a squeeze and it wouldn't have worked anyway as you can't sleep and giggle helplessly at the same time.

At home I always sleep naked and it's certainly warm enough to do so in here. The floor is nicely padded and aside from the slope it's just great. I'm asleep in minutes, exhausted, replete and content. Apparently Jen felt the same and nodded off minutes after me. If it's like this every day we're going to have a ball.

THE SECOND DAY OF THE CLIMB

"This morning we discerned the Mountains of Jagga more distinctly than ever; and about ten o'clock I fancied I saw a dazzlingly white cloud. My guide called the white which I saw merely 'Beredi', cold; it was perfectly clear to me, however, that it could be nothing else but 'snow'".

Given the sheer scale of Kilimanjaro, it seems incredible that it remained unknown to the world until German Johann Rebmann wrote this entry in his diary on 10 November, 1848. When he published his sighting the following year, modern science ridiculed the apparent discovery of snow on the equator. It took another thirteen years for the sighting to be confirmed, when snow fell on another German, Baron Karl Klaus von der Decken and his British geologist Richard Thornton at around 4,000m.

There is a great story that, in 1886, Queen Victoria moved the border between British and German East Africa to give the mountain as a birthday present to her cousin, the future German Kaiser Wilhelm. As she also owned Mount Kenya, he allegedly pointed out, it was only fair that he had Mount Kilimanjaro. The generous queen supposedly agreed. The true reason that Kilimanjaro resides in Tanzania and not Kenya is more to do with diplomatic negotiations than royal decree. That the story still survives is a tribute to the seemingly arbitrary splits imposed by Europeans on their conquered lands.

Many further attempts to scale Kilimanjaro reached higher and higher up the mountain before it was finally conquered. Hans Meyer and Ludwig Purtscheller are generally credited with the first ascent of Kilimanjaro, although their local guide Johannes Kinyala Lauwo is now reported to have beaten them to it some years earlier. Hans, a

German geologist and Ludwig, an Austrian mountaineer, reached the summit on 6 October 1889, Ludwig's 40th birthday.

We wake up at 6.30 after a peach of a sleep. I can vaguely remember peeling myself off Jen and crawling up the slope a few times in the night. Jen has also had a good night's sleep so I obviously didn't crush her too much.

It's bright outside the domed ceiling of the tent and we can hear the chatter of the porters below us. It's fresh and sunny when we emerge at 7am. I put my walking clothes out to dry a little longer as they are still damp from yesterday. John and Andy emerge stiffly.

"That was a dreadful night", groans John. "There was a massive tree root right across the middle of our tent."

"It wasn't that bad", says Andy. "It wasn't as comfortable as my own bed but we're half way up a mountain. What do you expect?"

"Well you must have had the good side. On my side it felt like I was lying over the summit."

"How did you guys sleep?" Andy asks us.

"Tip top", I reply, smiling.

"Pretty good", says Jen.

"Bastards", grumbles John.

Andy wanders off to the toilet with a "stop moaning" thrown towards John.

"I'll choose which side I sleep on tonight then", says John.

"You can choose tents if you like", offers Jen, rather more generously than I might have been.

"Nah, it's alright", says John. "You wait and see what it looks like when they take the tent up."

Breakfast is ready at 7.30, after which Jen and I spend a good ten minutes jumping up and down on her bag to make sure that the sleeping bag and roll-mat fit in and it zips up properly. It's almost harder work than the climb.

My clothes are cold and still damp when I put them on again. They probably smell too. I'm keeping my dry and warmer clothes for when we stop at camp, reasoning that the damp stuff will soon warm up and be damp again pretty quickly anyway. It takes a few minutes for my body to turn the cold sweaty t-shirt into a much more bearable warm sweaty t-shirt.

The porters pitch camp remarkably quickly. Our tents and bags are packed into sacks and loaded together. John stamps the ground where the tree root is supposed to have been.

"Look at that!" he says.

It's more a ridge of earth than a massive tree root and we try to hide our lack of amazement. He spots that we're not impressed.

"Well, it felt bloody uncomfortable to lie on, that's all I can say."

"Is he still whining?" says Andy.

Some of the porters head off ahead of us before Limu calls us to go. The path out of the camp is straight up and single file, and we're stuck behind a train of porters and South Africans. Extrapolè polè is the only option. We've not seen the Canadians.

"Did you enjoy the football the other night?" asks a South African voice with a slightly mocking tone.

"Yeah yeah yeah", replies John. "How did South Africa do?"

"We'll be there next time."

"It's easy when you don't have to qualify", says Andy. South Africa will host the 2010 Football World Cup and so will automatically qualify for the finals.

The banter continues up the steepest part of the climb so far. The vegetation has completely changed. What was thick, dense and dark green forest yesterday quickly becomes a wispy and light green bush barely 12 feet high. The South Africans pull away from us as the initial steepness eases off at the top of the ridge. The path is now firm underfoot and well-defined between the trees. The ground under the trees is completely covered in moss. The trees are all covered with what looks like the hair of an Afghan hound. Jen thinks it looks like the clouds have been caught in the trees.

The summit appears between the trees, a seemingly ridiculous distance away beyond the velvet folds of the valleys below us. There are a few small clouds floating over the top of the snow, drifting slowly through the bright blue sky. Every now and then the trees clear to the right and we can see into the depths of a very tall, thin, green velvet valley.

The cloud trees end at the foot of a vertical rock-face. The South Africans are waiting at the base while a picnic table and chairs are hauled up by a chain of porters. The Canadians are just behind them and we all watch and wait together.

"Did you sleep well?" I foolishly ask Abby.

"I didn't sleep at all", she replies. "I laid awake, like, the whole night. Our tent was on a thirty degree slope and there were rocks everywhere."

"It was quite basic", I sympathise.

"Aw, we had an enormous tree root under our tent", says John. "It kept waking me up all night."

"We were, you know, the furthest from the toilets too", she continues, ignoring both of us.

"Probably a good thing", I say. "How about you, Bear? Sleep well?"

"Here and there."

"He slept, like, all night", says Abby.

"We were talking a few times in the night", he says, gently, "and I got you some tablets another time."

Abby doesn't respond. She pulls some trail mix from her pocket and rams it into her mouth.

"Did you have any breakfast?" I'm really on form with my questions today.

"Hey, I'm not risking it. I'll stick to the food I've brought."

The table and chairs have cleared the rock face and the South Africans are making their way up with the help of their guides. We all shuffle forwards. Some porters have joined the queue behind us.

The South Africans make light work of the rock. Not so the Canadians. We let some porters through first, then wait for a good fifteen minutes while Abby makes the climb look as difficult as a person possibly can. She is eventually pulled up by a porter while Bear pushes from behind.

We let a few more porters through. A gas bottle is passed up, along with open wicker baskets, water bottles and more chairs. The porters are all in good humour, smiling and laughing as the heavy loads and ridiculously out-of-place items are passed from hand to hand up the near-sheer face. When our turn comes, our ascent is pretty rapid. Limu goes first, followed by Andy, then John, Jen and me. Jen has to stretch the most and still manages to make light work of it. There are plenty of handholds and the old advice of "don't look down" helps.

The Canadians are still sitting at the top when we get there.

Abby is sitting on a rock and recovering. Bear is standing a few feet away, admiring the stunning view of the valleys and mountain and seemingly unperturbed by Abby's potentially near-death condition.

We make polite comments about the difficulty of the rock face, wish them good luck for the rest of the walk and continue on our way. The vegetation has thinned out considerably and the mountainside has opened out ahead of us. Some of the bushes are still over head height but there are large gaps between them. The green of the plants has changed again, becoming brighter and darker than the faded look of the cloud trees below. We pass the South Africans, who have stopped for lunch in a small clearing.

I stop to put on my sun-hat and some sun-cream. The hat, a purchase from Byron Bay, Australia, some 6 years ago, was the widest-brimmed hat I could find at the time.

Ginger hair + direct sunshine = sore red face with a few more freckles.

Ginger hair + direct sunshine + wide-brimmed hat = smiley white face.

Simple really.

The strangest trees suddenly appear all around us. Limu calls them senacias. They are mainly brown, standing straight up from the ground and with a green flourish at the top. They look like someone has stood human sized sausages on their ends and placed a pot plant on the top of each one. They come in all sizes from little footballs at our feet to towering beasts twice our height. Some of the plants have split into two part-way up their trunk, with each branch having a green pom-pom at its end. The whole effect is not unlike the Joshua trees in the Californian park of the same name.

We stop for lunch on a rocky clearing above a small cliff face. The clouds below have cleared enough for us to see the dark forests around the base of the mountain give way to the khaki of the African plains stretching away to the horizon. There is barely a cloud above us, and behind us the top of Kili is blindingly white in the sunshine. We eat our lunch with the mountain at our back and devour the view below. It helps to distract me from the egg.

After lunch we all take photographs of ourselves, first with the mountain behind, then with the plains behind. It is impossible to capture the scale of what is around us. The height of the mountain and the expanse of the plains fail to make an impression on the one-inch digital screen of my camera. Even on Andy's two-inch screen and Jen's two-and-a-half inches, it is clear that the pictures are going to be somewhat inadequate. Still, you have to try.

Limu tells us that the camp is just two hours away and that the steepest part of the day is over. It is not even one o'clock and the prospect of arriving mid-afternoon and lazing in the sunshine fills us all with extra energy. Within half an hour we see the camp, a distant speck on a rocky shelf in front of the mass of the mountain. This is one of the most awe-inspiring sights so far. The tiny specks of tent provide the first frame of reference against the sheer size of the mountain. Until now the mountain has been a big rock in the distance. Now, relative to the tents, it is truly immense and actually difficult to take both in. If you look at the mountain, you struggle to find the tents again because you are not looking for anything that small. When you finally find them, you are once again overwhelmed by the immensity of the mountain above them.

As we wind our way towards the camp, the senacias become rarer and the vegetation drops to waist height, then knee height and eventually ankle height as we walk into camp at just after two o'clock. We're first here from our previous camp, beating all the colonials despite them setting off ahead of us. Did we walk too fast? It didn't feel that way.

We've climbed 1100m today, more than the height of Snowdon. Our camp for the second night is Barranco Huts, 3950m above sea level. We passed the huts on the way into camp. There are just two of them, both round and quite small. It's not clear to me who stays in them. Thankfully not us, I thought, as we could smell the odour coming out of the doors as we walked past. Give me a tent with my own smells any day.

At Barranco we have joined the South Circuit Path, so from here on it won't be just us and our porters on the trek. We will now have trekkers from the Shira, Lemosho and Machame Routes alongside us. These routes enter the camp from the north-west and the trekkers stay towards the back of the rock shelf. The Umbwe Route enters from the south and we camp near the front, meaning that we can spend tonight in relative isolation.

Jen has a snooze in our tent while we three boys sit out in the sun on the plastic patio chairs that the porters have brought for us.

It is, quite simply, a glorious feeling to have completed the walking for Day 2. It is crisp and warm in the sunshine. There is a bite to the air when a breeze does come our way and there is a bite to the sunshine that feels like we are being micro waved. I keep my fleece and hat and trousers on for protection.

We watch the South Africans arrive a little after us and wave at them. They are camping a few hundred yards away. Other than the dining tent there are no tents within a hundred yards of our two yellow domes. Large ravens stalk around the dusty ground, watching and waiting for us to leave anything interesting lying around. Our waiter comes over and warns us not to leave our bags unguarded, especially with anything shiny showing.

An afternoon tea of popcorn, peanuts and Milo arrives. Jen joins us, still feeling exhausted. We talk very little. I suspect that we are all feeling the effect of the altitude in some way and don't want to be the first to admit it. My head is a little sore and my stomach is gurgling away more heavily than I've ever known it – both conditions associated with altitude. A headache combined with another symptom is a classic indicator of altitude sickness. A rumbling belly is caused by the reduced air pressure allowing the gases in the stomach to expand. At least I hope that's the cause. Maybe Abby was right and I've been struck down by food poisoning from the packed lunch? Maybe. It doesn't make me hold back on the peanuts and popcorn.

After tea I head over to the toilet block to see if there are any ill effects. The toilets here are solitary wooden boxes the size of a telephone box. There is a door, one improvement on the previous camp, but no plug for the hole in the ground. Unlike the damp, dark toilets at Umbwe Caves, these toilets are baked, arid and windswept. The wooden walls are cracked and brittle rather than moist and crumbly. I'm pleased to manage two small poos, my first on the mountain. Apparently no food poisoning yet then.

The camp is enclosed on three sides. A ridge sweeps high above us to the left, the Barranco Wall rises vertically to the right and the mountain joins the two behind us. In contrast the ground in front of us drops away, disappearing into wispy clouds before it fully reaches the distant plains. The sun sets behind the ridge to our right. We watch the shadow creep across the ground towards us and then up the Barranco Wall on the opposite side. The air immediately turns a lot colder, so we take shelter in our tents until being called for supper at 5.30. It is now distinctly cold. To everyone's amusement, particularly the porters, I put on my alpaca fur hat that I bought in Cusco for the Inca Trail walk last year. It is more of a helmet than a hat, white and with fur that is about two inches long. At the time I bought it, everyone in my group thought I was mad or showing off or both. I think they continued to think this when I wore it on the first night of the trail, until one of them tried it on for a laugh and found it beautifully warm and comfortable. By the end of the trail, most people had at least tried it and liked it. Four of them even bought one before they left Cusco. The rest could never see when they would ever wear one again. Indeed a couple of people offered to take mine off my hands for the very reason that I could surely never find another occasion to wear it. Although I have yet to walk down a London street wearing it, it has had its uses. It was excellent when an Ice Bar briefly opened in London and it is jolly nice on bonfire night each year. It's also travelled to Krakow with Jen on a girl's trip and been up the snow-covered Derbyshire peaks. I can't wait to go skiing again.

Over a supper of pea soup, rice and vegetable goo and mango (not forgetting the Milo, of course), we admit to our general tiredness and ailments. Jen is feeling sick. John's got sore legs. Andy is suffering from sunburn. I've still got a faint headache. We are all knackered. Andy produces a pack of cards and the boys teach us how to play Shithead. It's good fun but darkness and tiredness prevent us playing more than one game. Although the sun set on our camp a long ago, it is only now setting over the distant and out-of-sight horizon. We are in bed by 7.30 and are ready for sleep. Jen pops an anti-sickness pill and we pretty quickly nod off. We wake up briefly at 11 o'clock, have a chat and then sleep right through until 6.30, when we are woken by a pack of braying South Africans.

THE THIRD DAY OF THE CLIMB

The name "Kilimanjaro" combines mystery and glamour with immensity and excitement, and its origins are similarly enigmatic. "Kilima" is the Swahili word for a "small mountain" (and sometimes "top of the hill"), and "njaro" is variously translated as "glittering", "shining" or "white" if you make the small side-step to ancient Swahili. (Some guide books also offer snow as a translation of njaro, although when I looked up "snow" in a Swahili-English dictionary it offered "theluji". An equatorial language having more than one word for something that barely exists in their locality seems as likely as there being more than one word for "sun" in English.) The explanation seems logical enough if you assume the locals had a cute sense of irony by naming the highest mountain on the continent "small". The Swahili name for a proper mountain is "mlima".

Other theories exist to explain the origin of the name. If you take "njaro", drop the n and switch to the local Bantu language of Kichagga, you get the word for "caravan". (This is not quite as surreal once you realise that the mountain is near the trade routes and it was no doubt a useful landmark for traders.) Switch to Masai and njaro means "spring" or "water". Or there's the kangaroo explanation: when travellers first asked the local Wachagga about the mountain, they replied "kilemajyaro", meaning "it's impossible to climb".

When Hans Meyer reached the peak, he ignored the arguments and did what all good Europeans would have done – he renamed it in honour of his monarch, Kaiser-Wilhelm-Spitze. The name for the peak (rather than the mountain) persisted beyond the middle of the 20th century although now the local name, Uhuru, is in common use.

Of course, most people now accept that the mountain was actually named after the rather excellent local beer.

The day is clear and crisp. Jen and I feel so much better than we did when we went to sleep. John and Andy are already up, as are the porters who are taking down their own tents.

"You're looking less pink there", I say to Andy as we join the boys at the breakfast table. I sit opposite John and Jen sits opposite Andy.

"I'm feeling less sore too", replies Andy, dabbing his face.

"Are you going to stop whinging about it then?" asks John.

"Shut up, fatboy", says Andy.

"I feel so much better today", says Jen. "I felt really bad last night."

The flask of hot water is already on the table, so I reach straight for the Milo.

"The Canadians have given up", says John.

"Have they?" say Jen and I together.

"Limu mentioned it when he came over. They left first thing this morning. Too tired."

"She should have eaten something more than trail mix and oat bars", I say, somewhat dismissively. I add a fifth heaped spoonful of Milo into my cup before starting on Jen's.

"I think if I'd still felt as bad this morning as I felt last night, and not slept as well, then I might have been heading down too", says Jen. "It might not have been Abby that forced them down, of course."

"I bet Bear's gutted", says John, as convinced as the rest of us that it's Abby who's wimped out.

"He probably just shrugged. Maybe he doesn't mind", says Andy.

"You've got to mind", says John. "If you'd come here and had to head down because your girlfriend wouldn't eat properly then you'd mind."

"I agree", I say, passing the Milo to John.

"I'd better eat my breakfast then!" laughs Jen.

"I bet she didn't drink Milo every night", says John, loading up his cup with 4 heaped teaspoons.

"And morning", says Andy.

"Not to mention tea-time", I add.

"The drink of champions", says John.

"Heroes!" says Jen. We all chink our cups of powder together before adding the hot water.

Breakfast is Milo, porridge, toast and fried egg. Fried eggs usually sit just below hard-boiled eggs on my list of least favourite foods, yet mixed with ketchup and toast they slip down and taste yum.

The waiter brings the big water container for us to top up our water bottles. Apparently this is the last of the water from the foot of the mountain. There is a water source at the next camp. Jen and I each have a 2-litre camel-pack, a clear plastic bladder attached to a long bendy straw with a valve at the end. You place the bladder in your day-pack, wind the straw over your shoulder and clip it on your collar, the idea being that you can drink whenever you want without having to stop and unload a water bottle from your day-pack.

I first saw them quite a few years ago on a trip up Ben Nevis, when two of my friends produced them at the foot of the hill. I thought they were the most ridiculous piece of hiking paraphernalia I'd ever seen and yet another example of the unnecessary tat that hiking shops sell to gadget-hungry trail-nerds. At the time my approach to hiking was to have a jacket with enough pockets to avoid the need for a rucksack at all. As my water bottle fitted into a readily accessible outer pocket, I wouldn't be stopping anyway if I needed some water. If I needed food, my macaroni pie and dinner-plate sized cornflake cake were in the opposite pocket (we were in Scotland, after all). Then a couple of years ago we attempted the UK Three Peak challenge – climbing the highest peaks in each of Scotland, England and Wales in 24 hours – and I finally saw in the tat what only, in my opinion, the gullible few had seen before.

Prior to the challenge and, in what can only have been a moment of weakness, I bought a camel-pack. As with any properly organised (rather than spontaneous "Ooh it's a nice day let's go for a walk") event, full scale health and safety considerations kick-in with a size 12 steel toe-capped boot. We were sent the list of essential items to carry in our day-packs up the peaks and it was clear that not even my generously pocketed jacket would cope. To ignore the list was to risk the fickleness of a (probably Scottish) kit-checker and be prevented from climbing the first peak because of a lack of a particular size of sticking plaster.

As it turned out, the organisers were right. The great thing about spontaneous walks is that they don't even cross your mind when there's dense fog, sleet and a gale-force wind at higher levels. When you're on a three-peak challenge and it's the first peak, however, you're going up the mountain in exactly those conditions if that's what the weather happens to be on the day. As well as the benefit of not having to pull a cold water bottle out of my jacket pocket to get some water, I also learnt that, despite profligate pockets, my jacket was not waterproof in horizontally-precipitous conditions. My normal t-shirt under a jacket and nothing else technique meant that I was soaked to the skin and shivering uncontrollably at the top of Ben Nevis. At one point on the way up I stopped for a wee and my hands were so numb that I couldn't feel my willy.

In addition to a waterproof jacket, warm fleece and camel-pack, other hiking tat that I fell in love with on that trip included walking sticks and ibuprofen. After successfully climbing Ben Nevis, I reached the bottom and found that my knees were incredibly sore, to the point that I struggled to even step out of the mini-bus. I was determined to at least try Scafell Pike as it was supposed to be the easiest of the three peaks. One of the team was ill by the time we reached the base, so she stayed in the van and I borrowed her walking sticks. Going up the mountain my knees were quite sore. As soon as I started to descend, I walked like a robot from a 1970's episode of Doctor Who. I literally couldn't bend my knees and was placing all my weight on the sticks just to keep going. Without them, I'd have been carried down the hill. After about an hour of the descending very slowly and painfully I realised that I was going to seriously struggle to get off the mountain. One of the team offered me some ibuprofen. I normally don't take any medication except in cases of imminent demise. The situation wasn't quite that serious but I was willing to try anything to avoid the humiliation of being carried off the mountain. I took the tablets and we carried on for another twenty minutes before stopping again for a drink and some chocolate. When we set off this time, I felt like I had new legs. All the pain, soreness and stiffness had gone. If I was religious and had prayed for help, the miraculous change in my legs would have been a defining moment of my life and a personal proof of the existence of God. As it was, I became a firm believer in the benefits of modern science, ibuprofen and walking sticks. In case you are wondering, I even managed to make it up Snowdon the next day and complete the challenge.

Back on Kilimanjaro, a mountain nearly twice the combined height of the three peaks, Jen and I complete the daily battle to fit our sleeping bags and roll-mats into our rucksacks. It's frustrating and exhausting, although thankfully we are about to set off on what we expect to be the easiest day of the climb. It's about 9.30 in the morning and the sun has been shining on our campsite for hours.

"How long will it take us", I ask Limu as we cross the camp.

"Three, maybe three hours", he says. "Polè pole."

"Polè pole!" we all repeat back.

"Heroes", cheers John.

Our first hurdle is to climb out of the rocky shelf of our campsite and up the Barranco Wall. The wall is a dark cliff on the opposite side of the campsite to that which we came in. The sun has yet to alight on most of it. As we cross to the back corner of the campsite we can see, along the path up the wall, the snaking lines of walkers who arrived via other routes and who must also have spent the night at the campsite. I notice that the campsite is slightly concave, so that from our tents at the front of the site we could not see over the curve of the ground to the larger numbers of tents at the back. There are a surprising number of people on the move and some of the groups are already a good way up the wall.

The path up the wall meanders back and forth, a single-file trail that is walkable aside from the occasional short climb. Each short climb is a bottleneck, where the progress of each group takes on the speed of the slowest person in all the groups. Everyone makes way for porters who also slow down to negotiate the tricky ascents. In contrast to similar hold-ups in our normal daily lives, people are good natured, happy to take their time and obey the polè pole tenet. Only once does a group, which seems to be generously endowed with slow and wary women, complain at us tailgating a team of porters past them. We apologise and polè polè on, never to see them again. Clearly everyone has their own interpretation of polè pole. For some there is an unspoken "very" in front of the phrase.

It is a long slog up the wall. Jen starts to feel queasy well before we reach the top. Although it is cold in the shade, I can feel my arms burning in the direct sunlight. Every time we wait while a bottleneck eases, I seek out an outcrop of rock and hide beneath it.

By the time we reach the top the sun is still not fully on the wall. Below us today, where yesterday we could see the plains, there is cloud right to the horizon. There is one break in the cloud; the peak of Mount Meru, itself some 5000m high. Limu says we must stop for a rest, so we take the usual round of pictures. (John in front of view, Andy in front of view, John and Andy in front of view, John in front of Kili, Andy in front of Kili, John and Andy in front of Kili. Repeat for Jen and me.)

The ground is brown and dusty and covered in small rocks, possibly deposited by the retreating ice now covering only the top of the mountain. The dusty soil covers a stark and volcanic terrain. Martians could land here and mistakenly think they'd arrived home. Other than a few meagre clumps of grass there is no vegetation. There is also little shelter and the light breeze makes it feel cold even as the sun burns our skin. Limu describes it as Alpine desert.

We've taken about 90 minutes to climb the wall, which means we should be about half way through the day's walk. Jen lays down against a rock in an attempt to reduce her sick feelings. It doesn't look like it is helping. She smiles up at me like a sick puppy wanting to be made well again. I resist the urge to pat her on the head.

"We go again", says Limu, after we've rested for 20 minutes.

Ahead we can see the path cross a low valley and disappear over and around a ridge. It looks like an hour or so's walk, which thankfully means that the camp must be just out of sight.

An hour later, we've crossed the low valley and the camp is not in sight. Instead there's another valley ahead, albeit much smaller than the last.

"Are we nearly there?" asks Jen. She's trying not to show it but she's really struggling now.

"Nearly", says Limu.

"How far is the camp?" I ask. "Is it just there?" I point to where the path disappears from sight over the next low ridge.

"We will see Karanga from there", nods Limu.

It takes us 15 minutes to reach the next ridge, which rolls away from us in a way that stops us seeing much more than a few metres ahead. We are all eagerly anticipating the camp when we summit the ridge and it begins to break ahead of us. We are not disappointed and then utterly disappointed. Not disappointed because, sure enough, we can see the camp not too far away; utterly disappointed because, between us and it, there is a deep, steep-sided valley. We've been walking for over 3 hours and there is evidently more than an hour still to go. We've not eaten since breakfast and it's taking its toll.

Well, for me that's the case. John and Andy's foresight to pack chocolate bars is sparing them a little. They offer us some of their supply, which Jen refuses immediately – she's feeling too sick to even look at what was offered. I also decline, even though I'm very hungry. I feel bad about taking their food when they've had the sense to bring it and the inconvenience to carry it. Silly really as they don't mind at all.

We crawl into Karanga Camp four hours and twenty minutes after setting off. Jen has done well not to puke in the valley of death. I need food but lunch is not ready yet. I momentarily feel annoyed, before remembering that our chef has also just walked the same path as us. He made our breakfast before we left too. Jen collapses into our tent which, as always, is ready for us. She's too tired to take off her shoes, never mind unpack her bag or make her bed. She lies in the middle of the tent with her feet sticking out of the door.

"I think I could sleep forever", she says.

I take off her shoes, blow up her bed and roll out the sleeping bag while she begins to doze. She manages to roll into the bag, which I zip up around her. I leave her in the tent and go outside to join the boys. They are already zipped up in their tent, also resting until lunch. The time is barely two o'clock and we are all done in for the day. I go back into our tent and find Jen fast asleep.

Lunch is a great surprise that cheers everyone. It's chicken and chips! How they cook the chips up here is anyone's guess but they taste fantastic. I have mine with vegetable goo, washed down with the obligatory Milo. Conversation is non-existent. We all try and be sociable but we are, quite simply, exhausted.

After lunch it's back for a lie down. I manage a poo on the way, which makes me feel better. I think we'd all imagined that we'd have a pretty chilled time here at Karanga Camp: a short morning walk followed by some lazing around chatting and reading. The reality is that none of us has the energy to socialise, and we all retreat into our own space to recover from the morning. The boys retire to their tent, Jen continues to seek out that extra bit of energy in the bottom of her sleeping bag, and I read a novel about a boy who shoots his family with a crossbow before turning it on his most-hated school colleagues and teachers.

Karanga Camp sits at an almost identical height to Barranco Huts. It's not that we haven't climbed significant vertical heights, it's just that we've also descended the same each time and so, despite all our effort, we've not even climbed any further up the mountain. There's still the same distance to climb as at the start of the day. This is all good acclimatisation, of course, so although it feels deflating it's simply as expected.

Amazingly some tours do not stop at Karanga but press on to Barafu, meaning that the trekkers would be attempting the summit tonight. If that was our tour I can safely say that none of us would be summiting. Before the trip, I read about the number of days you need to climb the mountain and the advice to take an extra day to acclimatise if it is offered. I also remember wondering how it would feel and whether it would be really necessary if you were fit enough. Today has been proof that it really matters.

Not that everyone needs the extra day. "Fastest ascent" attempts are frequent and, at the time of writing, the record time to reach the summit from one of the park gates is held by Sean Burch, a fitness consultant from Virginia. In June 2005, he made the journey from Marangu Gate to the summit in 5 hours, 28 minutes and 48 seconds. His training regime included skipping with rope at the top in the days leading up to the attempt. A small consolation for us mere mortals is that, having completed his task, his legs collapsed, he promptly threw up and then took a further 8 hours to get back down.

We eat a dinner of fried bread and pea soup, pasta and vegetable goo, and mango. And Milo. Everyone is a lot livelier than at lunch and we play cards until the light fades. For me the length of walk without any food was a real problem. For Jen it's the constant feeling of imminent vomiting. Andy's sunburn has abated although he's got a headache. John, like me, is tired but generally OK. Having eaten everything that's been put in front of us, we all go to bed. It's 7pm.

THE FOURTH DAY OF THE CLIMB

Finding snow barely 200 miles south of the equator is somewhat surprising until you remember that the peak is nearly four miles above sea level. It is a fact that the glacial coverage of the slopes and summit plateau has significantly decreased since Meyer's day and, if current trends continue, the distinctive white top will be no longer. What is not so clear is exactly when the glacier will evaporate its final drop and what is causing it.

At the beginning of the 20th century, more than twelve square kilometres were permanently covered with snow and ice. By the beginning of the 21st century this has depleted to less than three. Although often sited as proof of global warming, a team from Innsbruck has now shown that it is reduced precipitation, not increased temperature, which is the main contributory factor. The snow might be melting a bit but the main problem is that it just doesn't snow like it used to. Of course this could also be caused by global warming but the "the world's warming, Kili's melting" story is not quite so simple any more.

An interesting aside to the Innsbruck team's research has been that they have been able to dispel local farmer's fears that, with the ice sheets gone, their water source and subsequent livelihoods will also disappear. The team's calculations of the amount of water held in ice at the top, coupled with their observation that only 20% melts and flows down the mountain, proves that there isn't that much water up there and what there is doesn't irrigate the farmers' fields anyway.

So how many more years of tropical snow are there left? Opinions vary, usually in line with the angle of story the writer is trying to give. Ice cores taken from the ice fields show a 12,000 year history. Global warming pessimists say the history will end by 2020. The Innsbruck team is more optimistic, with an expectation that there will still be glaciers on the mountain over 40 years from now. Regardless, no-one is predicting a white Christmas at the turn of the next century.

Today is a short day and a very, very long day. It should be the shortest walk so far and yet, at midnight tonight, we will start our final climb to the summit. Let's eat the elephant in chunks, as an old client of mine used to say, and deal with the short day first.

The routine is pretty familiar now. Awaken at around 7.30, breakfast involving Milo at around 8, expend vast amounts of energy and thoroughly frustrate ourselves packing our bags at around 8.30, faff from around 9 until Limu gathers us to start walking at around 9.30. The scenery and terrain are a repeat of yesterday – no vegetation and lots of dust and rock. The weather is also identically clear, with wispy clouds floating across the top of Kili away to our left. It's a short walk to Barafu Huts involving an up, a gentle down and a final up to camp, taking us just 3 hours and forty minutes. At the top of the first "up" we pass a group of eight English women and one Englishman. They look and sound like a church mums group on a Sunday stroll with the vicar. My money's on not all of them making it to the top. At the foot of the final "up" we pass a group of people speaking French while eating their sandwiches. One of them, slightly apart from the group and not joining in their conversation, catches my eye. I respond and wish him good luck for the game tonight. France will be playing Portugal in the semi-final of the World Cup at 8pm local time.

"Thanks", he says in a not very happy, very English, accent. "I'm trying not to mention the bloody World Cup."

"Oops, sorry", I say and carry on past without another word.

We pass the South Africans a few times along the way and they pass us one final time as we pause for breath up the final slope. The final member of their group is straggling behind the rest, and we set off alongside him for the final walk into camp.

"You guys are pretty fast, hey?" he says.

"Really?" I reply, a little worried that we've perhaps been pushing things a little too much. "I thought we were polè polè perfection."

"Well, we've been trying to shake you guys off for the last 4 days and you beat us every time," he replies.

"No! We've been taking it as slowly as we can in case we don't make it to the top", I say. I can't even remember seeing them yesterday but that's probably because it was such a grim day.

He tells us there are five of them, all early forties and all very determined to reach the top.

"We'll see you there", I shout after him as he presses on ahead to catch up with the rest of the South Africans.

We arrive at Barafu Huts at just after one o'clock, eleven hours before the final push. The camp is at 4600m, meaning we've climbed 600m today. Strangely it was far easier than the zero height gain we made yesterday.

There are two camps where most people stop the night before the ascent. Kibo Huts, on the Marangu and Rongai Routes, is at 4700m and directly west of the summit. Barafu Huts is also at 4600m on the South Circuit Path and south of Kibo, although there is no direct path between the two camps. Whereas Kibo has many huts for trekkers to sleep in, Barafu has just two round huts, identical to those at Barranco except for the two lines of washing that are hanging outside this time.

Barafu camp sits atop a ridge that slopes away from the summit at a fairly steep angle. Well, steep for a campsite. The site slopes in two directions, which probably means that when the weather is bad, you can gain some natural shelter on one side or the other. Tents are dotted around it wherever sediment has settled between the rocks to form a large enough flat area. There are few sites where more than one tent can share the same piece of rock-free ground and we seem to have one of them. It's a fair hike to the toilets though.

We've got used to the toilets now. They all come in roughly the same form; a rickety, wooden, phone-box sized cubicle with a hole in the ground to squat over. Sometimes there are two attached to each other and generally each has a door of sorts. The ones here at Barafu are much the same, apart from one block that stands out as a must-try event. It's a block of three that looks like it arrived in the last week and it has a host of new features we've not seen on the mountain so far. The whole block sits on a concrete base; the wood is new and un-weathered; the doors fit perfectly and are all attached; each door has a shiny handle; and the block is all topped off by a baby-blue roof. As I walk over to try one out, I'm half-expecting an attendant to open the door for me and hand me scented towels.

Inside, the encrusted remnants of previous occupants show that the block didn't arrive last week. It's still pretty clean, although the solidity of the cubicle does mean that there is less ventilation, a vital ingredient when you're standing over a mini poo-mountain.

Walking back from the toilets I notice why we have a new block. About 20 yards away there is a cubicle that has blown over. The hole that it sat over is surprisingly shallow, but then this high up a mountain it's more surprising that a hole can be dug at all. The cubicle is barely 5 metres from the edge of large cliff. If anyone was in it when it blew over … well, let's hope that toilet cubicles falling over with people in them is the preserve of Carry On films.

Lunch is ready as I arrive back at the tents, which is great as we can then relax all afternoon until dinner. Jen is feeling dreadful and sleeps right through, falling asleep as soon as lunch is over and only waking when we are called for dinner. I feel apprehensive about getting enough sleep and having a poo at some point today, and to occupy my mind I carry on reading about the child psychopath. John and Andy are struggling in their own way and are similarly lost in their tent and their own thoughts. Dinner is a big pot of vegetables and potatoes and as usual we finish the lot. Nobody in this group is going to fail to reach the summit through lack of eating.

At this point I feel remarkably good and, in general, have done all the way. Sure, I breathe pretty heavily as I walk along but I've not got a headache and have no upset stomach other than a bit of extra rumbling and a bit more of a struggle to poo. The odd headaches that I have had along the way, usually when we set off after a break, have lasted barely a minute. So far I feel pretty lucky with my body's reaction to altitude.

Jen, on the other hand, is undergoing a personal nightmare. She is constantly waiting for the moment when she will throw up, which she feels is only a matter of time. She has a headache all the time and is taking anti-sickness tablets twice a day. Sleep helps, so she's resting and sleeping at all available opportunities. Most of the time there is little choice – she stops and falls asleep. Eating doesn't help directly – when you want to puke it's not high on the list of priorities – but it is no doubt helping to keep her strength up. If she makes it to the top then it will all have been worth it, and there is no doubting her determination to reach the top. If she doesn't make it, well, let's cross that little problem if it arrives.

John is coping. His legs are still sore and he's tired, although like Jen I suspect he's never going to admit many external signs of weakness. Unlike with Jen, I can't ask him directly and obtain an honest and unfiltered answer. I wouldn't be surprised if he's struggling more than he's prepared to admit, although maybe it is his natural reservation that is making him a little quiet. It's fair to say that we are all a lot less lively than when we first met.

Andy is possibly the best of all of us. Apart from a touch of sunburn and the breathlessness that affects us all when we walk any distance, he appears to be largely symptom-free. He's also quieter than at the start, and I doubt that anyone is being 100% honest about how they are really feeling. After our experience with Abby, no-one wants to be the whinger of the group. Neither does anyone want to be arrogant; the toughest test is yet to come, of course.

The common factor amongst us all is our simultaneous eagerness and apprehensiveness to begin the final ascent. With dinner over by six o'clock, there are far too many and far too few hours until we begin walking again.

Straight after dinner, Limu sits down with us and gives his final briefing. We will be woken at eleven for a midnight start. Supper will be ready for us. We must not drink milk, as it is not easily digestible at this altitude. (So much for not drinking it since we arrived in Kenya!) The weather looks like it will be kind, although it is impossible to predict the wind with any certainty and it is the wind that causes problems here. Rain is not a problem, we are told, and neither is snow. Wind is the enemy. It is difficult to walk against, and the wind chill makes the walk much more dangerous. We will only really know the wind when we reach Stellar Point, an hour from the summit. The aim is to reach Stellar Point by dawn. Limu refuses to be drawn on any more specific times than this. Aren't we supposed to be at the top at dawn and watch the sun rise from there? What time is dawn, exactly? He ignores us and carries on. We will stop briefly at Stellar Point, then carry on for the summit.

"Do you think we will all make it to the top?" asks Jen.

"I have taken 80 people this year. Only 2 did not reach the

top", replies Limu.

"What happened to them?" asks Jen, as quick as a flash.

"One was an American lady", says Limu. We all nod in an understanding way, as if this was explanation enough.

"She struggled all the way from the gate", continues Limu, "and did not even try for the summit. The other lady made it as far as Stellar Point and did not want to continue. She said that that was further than she had hoped to get."

Limu shrugged, as if he didn't really understand such an attitude but had little choice other than to accept the decision of a client.

"If I'm still conscious then I'm not stopping until we get to the top" says Jen.

"Heroes", says John.

"So have we done OK so far?" asks Jen, continuing to press her point.

"You are all good. There is no problem", Limu says.

He continues running through our itinerary. We will spend no more than 5 minutes at the top, then come straight back down to Barafu. We will eat here, sleep for an hour, then carry on down to the final camp at Mweka.

All plans beyond the summit drift past me. If I make it to the top, right now I don't really care what happens afterwards. Never in my life will it be truer that it's all downhill from that point on.

Walking poles are essential, says Limu. The boys are still sceptical. They've carried them in their backpacks all the way so far, refusing to accept that they might make the walk a little easier. Limu, though, is very firm. We must take them and use them. The scree slope that we will walk to the top is difficult and steep. Reluctantly the boys agree. Maybe it is the change in Limu that makes them acquiesce. This evening he is much less laid-back and much more directive. This is no longer simply a walk in the park, all friends together amidst much jollity. Limu is in charge and we will do as he says.

We must also wear gaiters. Again the boys question him – they've not been needed so far. Again Limu is firm. On the way down, without gaiters, your boots will fill up and we do not want to keep stopping to empty them. Out-reasoned again, they both agree.

We will not eat on the walk. We will need one, maybe one and a half litres of water. This seems bonkers to me. We will be walking for about ten hours with nothing to eat and only a litre of water to drink? I've drunk two litres each day so far and the walks have mostly taken less than half this, and been much less strenuous. As for not eating, how will we maintain our energy? Limu explains that we will not easily digest food at the higher altitude. He has checked what food we have returned each mealtime and says that we have eaten well. We will not need food. I secretly decide to pack something just in case. I've a reputation for becoming grumpy if I'm hungry and I don't want to become a miserable old boot when we're on top of the world.

Limu continues. We must wear two pairs of thick socks, two pairs of gloves, wind-proof trousers over our normal trousers and a water-proof jacket. It feels a bit late to be running through the finer points of the kit list for the first time and we're all pretty grateful that he mentions nothing we haven't already thought about and have in our bags.

"Heroes", says Limu as he leaves us. Was that a smirk on his face?

It's 6.30, just four and a half hours until our wake up call and time to get some sleep. I need to stop for a wee on the way to the tent and have a hankering for one of the good old rickety toilets. Good ventilation is not to be sniffed at. I find one on the opposite side of the ridge to the new block. It is built over the slope of the mountain, which means that one side is resting on the ground while the other is precariously propped up on some wooden supports. The drop (if the toilet collapses) is not too severe on this side of the ridge, although I still gingerly test the platform as I walk onto it. It has no door and one of the walls has partly come away, exposing the user to Kilimanjaro on one side and the route down to the plains on the other. It must be one of the best views from a toilet anywhere in the world.

Back at the tent, no sooner have I stripped off and burrowed down into my sleeping bag than I find I need another wee. I ignore it and cuddle around Jen. She is already dozing but sleepily reminds me to put anything that might freeze into the bottom of my sleeping bag. Bother. One of the many pieces of advice we read before we came was that it gets very cold at this camp, and that anything important should be kept warm by tucking it into the bottom of your sleeping bag. I rummage around and put my camera, contact lenses, head-torch and spare batteries in my sleeping bag. Another concern I picked up from reading websites is that batteries last for no time at all in the extreme cold at the top. Keeping them as warm as much as possible will preserve their life. I have spare head-torch batteries but my camera has its own rechargeable type that I'm risking will last the entire walk. It's doing OK so far, but what if it fails at the top? I'll be more than a little gutted. I put the thought out of mind and settle down once more to find that I half-need a poo. Bother again. I try and ignore it but, combined with the need for a wee, it just won't go away. I'm also thinking that I don't want to find I need a poo in the middle of the walk up the mountain. It's still not quite fully dark, so with my headtorch on, loo-roll in hand and wearing my boxer shorts and a fleece I scurry out to the toilet with the view.

Of course, once I get here I don't need one. I try squatting in all manner of positions to coax it out. Squatting in the box, squatting outside. Standing up, half-squatting, squatting with my knees around my ears. Headtorch on, making sure I hit the hole, headtorch off, so that the whole camp can't see my acrobatics. Finally the tiniest turd squeezes out and I can return to the tent a hero. Jen is still awake when I get back, and we both lay awake for what feels like hours.

We discuss whether sex would be a good way to make us sleepy but decide that energy preservation is much more important. If we join the three-mile-high club but fail to make the top then we won't be happy. Anyway, after four days of sweating our way through any number of different environments we're also far too filthy.

Next I fret about what exactly I'm going to wear. I decide on most of it – two pairs of thick socks, walking boots, gaiters, thermal long-johns, walking trousers, wind-proof trousers and boxer shorts, two pairs of gloves, thermal vest, t-shirt, fleece, balaclava around my neck (able to be pulled up if required) and alpaca hat on top – but cannot decide between my waterproof jacket and my down jacket. I decide to wear the down jacket. Then I remember that Limu advised us to wear a waterproof jacket, not mentioning down, (I should have asked, I know) so I decide to wear the waterproof one instead. I wonder if it will be very cold, so decide to wear the down one after all, with the waterproof jacket in my daypack just in case. But then it has to be daft to carry a spare coat up the mountain. I just need to decide on one and stop worrying about it. But which one? And isn't this where I started all this fretting?

Through the soothing background babble of voices of unknown origin there is the harsher sound of a radio with a football commentary. Someone is listening to France vs Portugal. As with the voices, I can't hear the words loud enough to discern the language, let alone what is being said. As I drift in and out of sleep I hear the commentary briefly become frenzied, suggesting a goal or a penalty.

We must have slept for a couple of hours when I wake up to the distant sound of the English ladies getting ready. Jen also awakens when, at 10.30, we hear a cheerfully British, female and middle-class voice ring out with "Everyone ready? Then let's go!"

Everything is quiet again once their footsteps retreat and this last half hour is the worst time. I know that the waiter will call us at eleven and waiting for the sound of his footsteps, in fact listening out for any sound, is like waiting for an executioner. It's a mix of dread for the final moment that's been approaching for days and relief that we'll finally be making our attempt on the summit.

At last, right on 11pm, the hangman arrives. We both scramble out of the sleeping bag immediately and get dressed. I find that the thermal vest I've brought is not long sleeved, something Limu specified at supper. Jen bought the vest and long-johns on eBay for £5 and, naively, we didn't think about long or short sleeves. I try Jen's spare. The arms fit well but the vest doesn't reach as far as my belly button, so I put mine over the top and the combination of the two is nicely snug. Down or waterproof? I opt for down with waterproof in the backpack, along with a change of t-shirt. I pack three litres of water (twice what Limu recommended at supper), two litres in the camel and two half-litres in water bottles. I just can't see how one and a half litres will last me ten hours. I also pack the liquorice that my mum bought me for the Inca trail and that I never used. (She had read that liquorice is good for altitude sickness and sent me some through the post. As with most liquorice, it contained gelatine which, as a vegetarian, I don't eat. When I told her, she went on an apparently long, wide and ultimately successful search of North Wales for some gelatine-free liquorice. What I eventually received were two, 1-metre long pieces of liquorice rolled up into a pair of flat circles. I took them with me to South America and never ate them, mainly because there was always so much better food around.) Maybe the summit of Kilimanjaro and our food ban will be their destiny.

All dressed, we scramble over to the breakfast tent for our second and last supper of the day. The boys are there already, dressed in their multitudinous layers of clothing and with balaclavas around their necks. There is no Milo due to the milk ban (is there milk in it?) so it's tea, biscuits, apprehension and excitement all round. John has perked up and looks a lot brighter than he did when we last saw him. Although not appearing to suffer earlier, Andy also appears cheerier. They both found sleep stubbornly hard to come by but still managed to drift off for two or three hours. With Jen also looking livelier, the upbeat mood makes me feel absolutely ready to be on our way. Supper is short and suddenly, after a quick check of the bags and a quick trip to the toilet, it's midnight.

THE FIFTH DAY OF THE CLIMB

The International Society for Mountain Medicine defines three Golden Rules to help you "enjoy the high altitude".

One: If you feel unwell at altitude it is altitude illness until proven otherwise.

Two: Never ascend with symptoms of Acute Mountain Sickness. These include a headache together with one of the following symptoms: loss of appetite, nausea, or vomiting; fatigue or weakness; dizziness or light-headedness, difficulty sleeping.

Three: If you are getting worse while at the same altitude (or have High Altitude Cerebral or Pulmonary Edema), descend at once. If you start talking rubbish or can't walk in a straight line, presume you've got HACE. If you feel any two of extreme fatigue, breathlessness at rest, fast, shallow breathing or a cough, possibly producing frothy or pink sputum, or if you exhibit any two of gurgling breaths, chest tightness, fullness, or congestion, blue or grey lips or fingernails, or drowsiness, presume you've got HAPE.

The Kilimanjaro Express is the name given to the rickety one-wheeled cycles that are used to rush the injured or unwell off the mountain. If ever there was an incentive to obey the golden rules, it's the thought of hurtling down the rocky paths on a metal framed bed with one wheel. If you felt unwell up the mountain, you would be guaranteed to arrive feeling exactly the same at the bottom.

As we stand waiting for Limu, the South Africans pass us on their way across the camp to start the walk. As always they are in good cheer and we all wish each other good luck with spirited calls of "See you at the top". The temperature in the camp is cold but not ridiculous. I've no idea whether it is above or below freezing – I'd guess it is a few degrees below. There's not a breath of wind, which is excellent, although no indication of what the conditions will be like at the summit. We can see the summit shining brightly in the moonlight and it doesn't appear to be in gale-force conditions at the moment.

Limu collects us a few minutes later and, after all the waiting and anticipation, we begin our polè climb to the summit. For many days we've seen the peak and yesterday, in the daylight, we saw the start of the walk. However we've not seen the large part in-between. In the darkness, with our headtorches, we can just about see the feet of the person in front. It's a cloudless night with a half-moon away over the ridge to the left. On another occasion I would have stopped to admire the sheer multitude of stars visible above us.

Limu described the walk to Stellar Point, one hour from the summit, as being a steep climb out of camp, followed by a level walk then a long, steep, zig-zag ascent. Patrick, the second guide, leads us, followed in a line by Jen, me, Andy, John and Limu. Patrick sets an extra polè pace so that we have little reason to stop. At these temperatures even stopping for a short rest is a risk. Sweat chills very quickly and in turn chills you, stiffening your muscles and making moving on again a lot of effort. The aim is to walk slowly enough to not stop at all.

Given our speed we're surprised to pass the South Africans within 15 minutes of leaving camp. Their cheery greetings this time are a little forced. We're beating them again and this time on the leg that matters, except that what really matters is who reaches the top. Despite our pace feeling very slow and measured, I hope that overtaking the South Africans so early doesn't mean that we've rushed out of the blocks too quickly.

The moon dips behind the ridge, or maybe we are more in the depths of the ravine we must eventually climb out of. Either way, the night gets much darker. As explained by Limu, the ground levels off for about half an hour before rising again. Above us in the distance we can see two groups of lights bobbing their way in the darkness. They look a long way away, both horizontally and vertically. The path quickly rises sharply and we plod up the scree, in headtorch-lit darkness, for the next four hours. Four hours!

Let's just put that in perspective for a moment. Sure, in the grand scheme of global exploration then we've not made an impression. In the grand scheme of my life it is quite tough. Try it for a moment. Go to the foot of your stairs, close your eyes and walk slowly to the top. It probably took you 10 seconds. Multiply that by about 1,500 and you're getting an idea. Now set your alarm for 1am, put a 5kg rucksack on your back, run around the block for an hour to get nicely out of breath, close your mouth and block one nostril, then walk the one flight (remembering to think at the top that you need to do that another 1,500 times). Add freezing temperatures, make your stairs descend at around half the pace that you're walking up to simulate the scree and add the odd stranger vomiting up their supper. Finally, add in the fact that you have little idea of how long you've been walking or indeed how much further you have to go and you are well on your way to having your very own Kili experience.

Of course, the four hours are not entirely without incident. In some ways it helps to relieve the monotony. Dotted along the way are the English women who set off an hour and a half before us. One by one they are dropping out or stopping for increasingly more frequent breaks. One or two of them look particularly bad and won't go any further, while others just look awful and will probably continue, for a while at least.

About two hours in (I'm guessing – who knows, really), Jen pukes. Right out of nowhere, she projects a stream of liquid off to the side of the path. We've kept our order on the path (Patrick, Jen, me, Andy, John, Limu), and we all stop in a line behind her as she sends another stream over the rocks. Limu pushes past us to check that she is OK.

"You will feel much better now", he says, and he is right too. Jen perks up considerably. She drinks some water, eats a small bite of liquorice and then Limu is urging us on almost immediately.

So far, my decision to wear the down jacket is proving to be a good one. The alpaca hat is also tremendous. My body is toasty warm all over apart from my little fingers which, even though they are each inside a thermal glove and a ski-glove, are both very cold. Holding the walking poles is probably not helping as my hands are generally out front and level with my elbows, making my circulation need to work that bit harder for the warm blood to reach them. I take both fingers out of the individual glove fingers and try to warm them against the palm of my hand. It helps a bit but, as the night wears on, they start to feel glassy and I have to bang them against my legs to get any feeling back. It's just an early and superficial stage of frostbite but it's bloody annoying that I can't get rid of it.

My only other discomfort is my lips. They are very sore and feel like the skin has cracked all around my mouth. Both lips feel encrusted with dry chapped skin and I have to keep licking them to stop them cracking further. How arctic explorers cope with bits of their body failing like this for weeks on end is anybody's guess. We've been going for a few hours and we are all desperately checking for any sign of dawn. Realistically it is still a long way off but you can't help hoping that you've been walking for longer than you have.

The higher we climb, the more our water freezes in our bottles. First it's the tubes for our camelpacks that freeze. Jen's water-tube freezes first. I suspect that she is drinking less frequently and so keeping the liquid less mobile, quickening the freezing process. I check her water-tube and try to unfreeze it and notice that her tube is made of a much thinner plastic than mine, providing less insulation from the chilled air. Thankfully she has probably been drinking after all. I fail to unfreeze her tube so we share mine for a while, which I manage to keep flowing by holding as much of it in my mouth as I can. I feel like a pelican with an eel in its beak. Next it's John's turn. His water freezes completely, so I give him one of the two half-litre bottles that I've moved into my coat and so closer to the warmth of my body. Eventually my camel-pack freezes too, so Jen and I sparingly share the final half-litre. This proves to be vital for both of us and especially Jen, who has vomited a lot of fluid and needs to replace it. Even when the middle of the bottle freezes, we manage to keep going on the dribbles that I've managed to keep warmer by regularly squeezing the bottle.

Jen, who has been doing an excellent job of setting a great pace for us all, starts to stop more frequently. This is a concern for three reasons. Firstly, it means that she's reaching the limit of what she can endure. Even with immense mental dedication, a point will be reached where her body can take no more. It goes without saying that we don't want to reach that point. Secondly, each time Jen stops, we all stop. Even though we are all grateful for the break, standing still in this temperature causes your body's temperature to plummet. Thirdly, each time she stops makes it more likely she won't start again.

Jen vomits again, this time with much less liquid to get rid of. She is really starting to struggle, so much so that she doesn't notice the 4-inch long glob of snotty puke hanging from her nose. I point it out and she wipes it away with a glove.

It's not just Jen that's struggling though. I'm extremely breathless and at each stop I put my weight over my poles and wheeze. The boys seem worlds away, even though Andy is just two paces behind. Andy seems the best and even has the presence to take a photo of the three of us. We gather around Jen. John struggles to get into the picture. We all dredge up a smile from somewhere. Click. Limu claps his hands; it's time to move on before we get cold.

We see some snow off to one side of the path, then more and more as we climb higher and higher. We're still looking for any hint of light that means that dawn is on its way. The darkness and scree seem interminable.

Jen pukes again and again we stop. Limu calls from the back of the group for us to carry on and not stop.

"We will freeze", he shouts impatiently.

Patrick says one word in Swahili back.

"Oh", says Limu, realising why we've stopped. Jen vomited less volume this time and he hadn't heard the splatter.

The situation is becoming critical now. The frequency of stops, the regular puking, the never-ending darkness and scree are all questioning whether or not Jen should continue. I think about asking if she wants to carry on and decide not to bother; I already know the answer. I think back to the debate we had before we even booked the trip. If one of us has to turn back at any point, what does the other do? Do they continue to the top or stay to look after the other? We both agreed that it was only fair for the well person to continue. It is, after all, the only rational way to proceed; the sick person will be well looked after, the well person won't be able to do anything to help and, most importantly, neither of us could face being the reason why the other failed to reach the top. Decision made. Yet here on the mountain, nothing feels entirely rational. If Jen has to stop now, can I really leave her behind. In the cold dark reality that we now face, the decision is not so easy any more.

Limu mutters something to Patrick, again in Swahili. Patrick mutters something back, then takes Jen's arm and we are off up the hill at the twice the previous pace. Either we'd slowed down and not noticed or we are now walking at double speed. I take Jen's poles so that she can use Patrick's arm more heavily. It's almost as if Patrick is dragging her up the hill. I'm not sure any of us can keep this pace up for long.

Suddenly, out of absolutely nowhere, the ground levels off and we pop up over the top of a ridge. There are other walkers standing and sitting around us. A sign on the rock to our left reads "Stellar Point, 5735m". I can't take in what has happened, and it takes a few moments for me to realise where we are and what we've just achieved. We've made it out of the valley. We've defeated the scree. Although it's not quite dawn, faint traces of blue on the horizon show that we have made it through the night. We've done it, we've done it, we've beaten this mountain that so nearly beat us! I want to jump up and down with the sheer emotional ecstasy of the achievement.

I fling my arms out from my sides and spin slowly around to savour the moment. As I turn back, I notice that Jen is sitting against a rock, in tears and taking a paracetamol. It's a sobering moment. I walk quickly over and hand her the water. She swallows it and then pukes it straight back up. She doesn't seem to care too much. I pat her head for want of something more useful to do.

Now that I'm a bit more back on planet Earth, I calculate that if we're at 5735m, then there are only 160 vertical metres left to climb to the top. The path ahead along the ridge looks so flat compared to what we have just climbed that I feel like none of us can fail. We've climbed the worst and it should be just a case of hanging in there for the final push. I look at Jen uncertainly and hope she feels the same. The boys are standing looking at the slowly breaking dawn, not speaking.

Limu calls us all to start on the final walk to the top.

"One hour", he says. It's 5.40.

Jen gets up and without me even asking her anything, she nods and forces a smile. She knows how close we were to failure. She also knows that, despite feeling the worst she's ever felt in her life, the worst is over. From the start we've both been keen that we both make it to the top. She's in no mood to do anything other than reach the summit with me. John and Andy come over to join us. Where a few minutes ago we were worlds apart, we are now the team of heroes once more.

Limu presses us on at a good pace. The change of slope and terrain, from steep scree to gentle earth, is heavenly. I feel elated and exhausted; I know I'll make it even though there is still a fair bit of work to do. It's the final mile of the marathon, where the fear of not finishing vanishes and you can finally enjoy the crowds and emotion of what you are about to achieve.

Daylight is chasing us from behind and we almost scamper along. We turn off our head-torches. We find ourselves with more and more snow around our feet. The mountain-top glacier appears to our left, bluey-white, and then some deep icy snow cuts across our path. It is quite difficult to negotiate. It is encrusted with ice and has formed knee-high peaks. The boys go ahead with Patrick and we trudge behind. Jen appears to be on autopilot. It is hard for me to lift my legs over the icy tips and it really slows down Jen. If a field of hot lava opened in front of us, I think she'd press on over it regardless.

Dawn finally breaks over us and upon the calm, beautiful mountaintop. Africa all around us is covered in cloud that looks like just another part of the glacier at our feet. There are many false summits where we think that this must be it, that we can't see any higher point beyond the closest ridge-top, only for the mountain to open up again ahead of us. Yet I don't feel demoralized. I know that it is now only a matter of time before the next summit is the final summit. Sure enough, just when I resign myself to another false summit, Jen points and says "It's the sign". I don't see it immediately, then think she must be hallucinating, then it's there, right in front of us, instantly recognisable from all the photographs. John and Andy are already almost upon it. We race the final few steps and I'm almost in tears. Well, alright, I am in tears. Jen is too. Neither of us can quite believe that we've both made it. I can't speak. I thought I'd done with my emotional bit at Stellar Point but here it is emotional all over again, only different this time. At Stellar Point, it felt like we'd beaten the devil in the mountain. Here at the summit we're with the angels. This is it, this is what we set out to achieve, and we're both here and smiling. Jen and I hug each other, two Michelin mountaineers in our down jackets. I shake John and Andy's hands and Jen hugs them both. Then we all hug each other. It's just a bit much for all of us really.

I remember that we must take some pictures, so we do about half-a-dozen each in front of the sign. My mum has given me a Welsh flag to carry to the top, so I make sure I have my picture taken waving it in front of the sign. (She also gave me a sew-on badge to stitch onto my rucksack but I thought that was taking patriotism a little further than was necessary.) I'm quite pleased I remember to get the picture with the flag. Jen is completely dazed and just does what I tell her. Stand there, smile, now take a picture of me, now come back in front of the sign for a picture of all of us, give your camera to Limu so he can take the picture, and so on. John also appears to be not altogether with us. Some more people arrive and want to take their picture in front of the sign, so we move away and have a few moments to take in the scene.

The view is stunning. We look down on the rising sun and the whole world that we can see below the mountaintop is covered in clouds. The cloud tops are some 2500m below us and some 2000m above the ground below that. Including us and our guides, there are maybe a dozen people around. The air is still and the sky above is blue and cloudless.

The sign itself looks exactly like the sign I've seen in numerous pictures of people at the top of Kilimanjaro; four planks of wood of uneven length bolted haphazardly onto two upright posts. Neat yellow letters cut into the wood read

---

CONGRATULATIONS!
YOU ARE NOW AT

UHURU PEAK, TANZANIA, 5895M. AMSL.

AFRICA'S HIGHEST POINT
WORLD'S HIGHEST FREE-STANDING MOUNTAIN

ONE OF THE WORLD'S LARGEST VOLCANOES.
WELCOME

It looks so rickety and makeshift and yet must withstand severe winds and weathering.

According to Limu, we arrived at the top at 6.42. We're in the first five or ten to arrive. (Later, on the way down, I met a French man who said he reached to top at 5.50 and was the first there. He said there was a woman ahead of him who would have beaten him but she fainted, twice, so he passed her and got there first. He was proud of his achievement too. I didn't ask him whether or not he thought to stop and help the woman, rather than leave her in a heap on the side of the path. It clearly hadn't crossed his mind.)

If it was a little warmer and we could breathe more easily we would have stayed longer to appreciate everything; the view, our achievement, the icy crispness of the air, the eerie crater. As it is, with the sun rising higher and more people arriving, Limu decides it is time to leave and head back down. I pause, a momentary pang of reluctance to leave. After all the effort and emotion to get here, it feels far too soon for it to be over. Then in a moment the feeling is gone and we're off. It's never the destination that matters, it's always the journey. And the journey isn't over yet.

Walking down and into the sun is surprisingly warm. We pass lines and lines of utterly exhausted people making their way to the summit. They look as knackered as we felt only a few minutes earlier. I don't recall passing anyone on the way to the summit but I realise that we must have. I cheerfully say hello to everyone and get a few grunts in return. I know how they feel. My cheeriness and obvious spring in my step probably doesn't help.

We reach Stellar Point in no time at all, where I assume we'll stop for a rest, a wee and a bite to eat. Limu doesn't even pause. He turns straight off the ridge and down the scree. Suddenly I'm not so full of energy.

Despite Limu's drive I pause briefly to take stock of where we are. Straight on is the Marangu Route down to Kibo Hut via Gillman's Point. A colleague of mine who had attempted the climb a few years ago made it as far as Gilman's Point before turning back. I had hoped, and even assumed, that we would also see it but this is where our routes part. I saw the pictures of his climb almost every shot was shrouded in dark grey clouds. He said that the wind at Gilman's Point was strong and many people stopped there. Today there is not even a breeze or the tiniest cloud above us. Truly perfect weather

Exhaustion hits me as I take the right-turn over the edge of the ridge and plunge down the scree. My legs almost buckle with the sudden steepness. Did we really walk up this? It looks even steeper than it felt in the dark. It's so sheer and slippery that the easiest way down is to ski over the gravel. Unfortunately, like with skiing, my legs begin to ache. I could really do with a rest for 5 minutes. In fact, why can't we stop and rest? I think we'd all feel better for it. I know I would.

John pukes, which pulls me out of my personal sorrow. I'm not alone in thinking that this is hard work. Jen and I take off our coats while he finishes vomiting. I breathe deeply and realise how hungry I am. I almost heave, and find that I have to keep my breathing shallow if I'm not to throw up too.

The scree goes on forever. Like the false summits as we climbed to the top, there are false bottoms as we descend the scree.

"Which do you like the least?" asks Limu, knowingly. "Climbing up the scree or coming down it?"

With the focus on reaching the summit, my assumption that, in all respects, it would all downhill from the top, is beginning to prove a little optimistic.

"Both", I reply to Limu. I so want to stop, rest, get some food inside me and get some energy back. At least our water has melted so that we can drink.

There is no option to stop. We will rest at Barafu for an hour and eat there. We carry on. Andy and Patrick go on ahead and eventually disappear into the distance, Jen and I carry on behind them and John and Limu bring up the rear a fair way behind us. Jen and I agree that this is one of the most hideous experiences of our lives. It reminds me of my one and only attempt at running the London marathon. For the last eight miles I was feeling terrible and just wanted to finish. The main factor that kept me going was the thought that, if I stopped or slowed down, it would take longer for the agony to be over. On that occasion I did keep going and eventually ran all the way to the end. Perseverance in the face of feeling utterly exhausted is what is called for again today. I stop near the bottom for a wee, scrambling off the path and hiding behind a large boulder. I can see Jen standing on the slope, staring sightlessly ahead. She looks like she might topple over at any moment.

After 5,400 seconds (I know, I felt every one of them) we reach the bottom of the scree. It is a huge relief but there is still a way to go to camp. There is actually a small climb out of the valley which means that on the way up we must have walked downhill for a short while. Neither of us can remember doing so. After the agony of the scree, it is easier to be going up again.

As we crest the ridge we can see Barafu camp just a short way below us. It's a great and welcome view. The camp is sparsely dotted with tents and toilets. The ridge on which it sits is a square, brown stump of a rock, rising away from us before dropping to a flat desert. I notice that the new toilet block is perched over the edge of the high cliff in a way I hadn't fully appreciated when I used it. We can see three other new toilet blocks around the camp that we hadn't seen before. Now with the camp and our tent in sight we are keen to press on. We don't stop to admire the view of Mount Mawenzi, the 5,149m high mountain away to our left.

"Impressive", I say to Jen.

"Isn't it", she replies.

We arrive at camp at 9.40 and are offered a choice of food then an hour's rest or vice versa. Jen, Andy and I know what we want first – rest – and we wait for John to make sure he's in agreement.

"Whatever", says John.

We're straight in the tent to get the rest. Jen and I look at each other and hug. We made it, so why don't we feel more excited about it any more? Jen looks done in. Her face has puffed up to the point where she looks like she's had collagen implants in her lips, cheeks and eyelids. Her eyes are narrow slits peeping out of the puffball lids that she can barely keep open any longer.

"Look at your lips", she says half-heartedly. "You look like you're wearing lipstick."

We don't have a mirror, so I take a picture of myself at arms length and have a look on the small digital screen. She's right, I have a thin red line of crusted blood outlining my lips. What I'd thought was dry skin cracking was actually dried blood. I look decidedly camp. The lips aren't sore, as such, just uncomfortable and if I smile too broadly they split again.

The hour slips by in a flash. Jen can still barely move and is undecided on breakfast or more sleep. I'm hank, as a friend of mine always says, so I'm definitely having breakfast. I offer to bring some in for Jen.

"No, I should come and join you", she says, without enthusiasm.

John and Andy are already tucking into the mushroom soup and toast when we arrive. Andy pours us each a serving while I dive into the Milo. They both look shattered.

"Everyone feel as knackered as me?" I ask.

Nods all round.

"We'd feel even worse if we hadn't made it", says Andy.

Everyone nods.

"We did make it, didn't we?" asks John.

Everyone nods again.

"Heroes", says Jen.

Everyone nods and smiles. We don't feel like heroes.

We're supposed to have packed our bags and removed them from the tent before breakfast but Jen and I were both too tired. I had hoped some food would perk me up. It's made little difference. We rush breakfast and go back to the tent to sort out the mess of used clothes and camping paraphernalia. Jen sits in the middle of the tent, takes a look around her and looks more dejected than I've ever seen her. I realise how much harder this has been for her than me. The nausea and headaches for days, the vomiting all night, the constant fatigue and the anxiety about whether or not she'd make it to the summit, the worry about not letting the team down, not being the only one not to make it, have all taken their toll. Not only has she kept it going to the top, she's also held it together enough to get down to camp as well. This is where it was supposed to end, where she was supposed to feel better. If her expression right now is anything to go by, she actually feels worse.

"My arms won't work", she says, flopping them up and down by her sides. If she'd had enough energy I think she'd have cried.

"Lie there", I say. "I'll pack the bags."

"You're tired too", she protests.

"If I ever look as tired as you do right now, you can pack my bag for me too", I say.

Packing down the four-season sleeping bags into their carry-bags and then the carry bags into the rucksacks is always a bit of a mission. This time, without Jen and without any energy, I feel like throwing it all out of the tent and just lying down too. Outside, a porter is unpegging our tent around us. I look out and he is smiling and apologising as he does it. It brings me back into focus. OK, he hasn't been to the top, but he does have to run down to the next camp with a huge bag on his back and put the tent up before we get there.

We finish packing the rucksacks – Jen helps quite a bit in the end as she's seen me struggling and failing to do it on my own. The tent almost comes down around us so we sort out our daypacks on the rocks outside. John and Andy's tent has long gone and they are sitting with their backs to us admiring the view. There's no time to relax for us though. My socks are missing – I must have packed them in the rucksack – so I chase after the porter who is rapidly disappearing with the rucksack. The socks are near the top, thank goodness. I get back to my boots to find Jen is having no luck tying her laces. She really doesn't have the strength in her arms to pull them tight. I quickly do them for her, then do mine, then Limu arrives to collect us. It's just after midday. I feel like I need another hour's rest.

Then within 2 minutes of leaving the camp, something quite remarkable happens. I suddenly feel perfectly well, not tired at all and in fact quite full of energy. I look at Jen and, although she still looks tired, she seems to have more of a spring in her step than I'd expected. I avoid saying how I feel for a few minutes, both in case the feeling passes and to not make Jen feel any worse. If anything, a few minutes later I feel even better. I stop to take an ibuprofen in case my knees start to hurt. So far they're fine and I want them to stay that way. Jen waits with me.

"I feel so much better all of a sudden", she says, slightly bewildered

"Me too!" I reply excitedly.

"Ten minutes ago I just wanted to be packed in the rucksack and carried down the mountain", she continues. "Now I think I could skip all the way."

"Bonkers, isn't it?" I say.

"I'm starving too", she says. "What have we got to eat?"

"Highland shortbread?"

"Ooh, yum!"

We call after the others and offer the celebratory shortbread around. Limu has never come across it before. He picks up on the word bread and says it's the nicest bread he's ever had. The boys also have some. They also look brighter. As if by magic, we all feel like heroes.

The walk from Barafu Huts to Mweka Camp feels, for the most part, like a straight short run down the mountain, which is exactly what it is. The reason why people don't climb the mountain this way is acclimatisation. If people ascended via the Mweka Route, the most direct route to the top, they'd not cope with the altitude. The other routes meander their way to the top to give walkers the chance to adjust to the altitude, and every extra day spent getting used to the altitude increases the chances of reaching the top.

Dotted alongside this descent route are abandoned, apparently broken vehicles. They look like a wire bed frame on a single bicycle wheel. Limu explains that they are the ambulances in case anyone gets hurt. I think he's joking, then look again and realise that the contraptions aren't broken, just very basic. The single wheel makes negotiating the rocks much easier, and the lack of any nods at comfort means it can sit out here on the hillside for years and still be ready for use. It's certainly a good incentive to get off the mountain under your own power.

We've spent days in the Alpine desert and yet it takes just an hour for us to be back in vegetation, albeit just scrubby grass. Another hour finds us in the trees and an hour after that we walk into Mweka Camp. Aside from the countless porters, on the whole route we only saw one other group of people, five Americans who we never saw before or again.

Mweka Camp is a clearing chopped out of the forest. It's been chopped out very well and has the feel of a campsite in the South of France. Whereas in France, hedges would be laid to give the campers some privacy and to line the paths around the camp, here the hedge-like trees have been left and the spaces cleared in-between. Each achieves the same effect; the only difference being that, in France, the perimeter hedge might be a metre thick; here it's tens of miles.

At 3100m, Mweka Camp is pretty much outside any possibility of altitude sickness, certainly on the way down when most campers have acclimatised. We've descended 2795m, more than twice the height of Ben Nevis, and we feel fantastic!

We sign in at the camp hut in the same way that we signed in at the Umbwe gate. The hut sells warm Coca-Cola and Kilimanjaro beer. We're tempted but decide to wait until we've completely left the mountain before starting the celebrations. Instead we are given afternoon tea (Milo) and biscuits in our dining tent, then the obligatory three-course dinner, this time of pancakes and mushroom soup, rice and vegetable goo, and orange quarters. Once we've eaten the pancakes, none of us are hungry and most of the rice and goo gets returned. The rejection does not go un-noticed. Limu comes in to check that we liked the food since we ate so little of it. We assure him that we are happy campers.

The toilets here are still the same wooden cubicles. On the exposed, cold and dry mountainside they are unpleasant enough. Here in the warm, damp forest they are rank. No poo encrusted walls here; the poo is still moist and covering the floor too. The walls are also moist and there's no breeze to waft the smells away. Glastonbury would be proud.

At 6.30 the light fades and we're all a little tired. (Only a little, note.) We didn't really sleep last night, after all (is it only 12 hours since we were on top of the mountain?). As we leave for bed, our waiter catches us and asks if we have any spare batteries for his torch. Jen and I give him three, which is all we have spare. He seems happy.

We gratefully crawl into our sleeping bags and fall straight to sleep.

THE SIXTH DAY OF THE CLIMB

Despite the large number of inexperienced climbers attempting the mountain and the tales of the horrible death that awaits those who fail to heed the warnings of altitude sickness, very few trekkers actually die on Kilimanjaro.

Three Americans died climbing the Umbwe Route in 2005, when a rockfall on the final night before summiting crushed them while they slept. This part of the Umbwe route, ascending via the Western Breach, was subsequently closed by the park authorities. On record, this incident was without precedent.

A more common cause of death is from acute mountain sickness, resulting in a high altitude cerebral edema (swelling of the brain) or pulmonary edema (fluid on the lungs), although actual statistics are hard to find. This is hardly surprising, given that the only people who hold a record are the Tanzania Park Authority, who are well aware that such statistics don't bring in the tourists.

Death rates for porters have traditionally been much worse than those for trekkers. An incident in 2002, when three porters died from extreme weather conditions that took a turn for the even more extreme, seems to have reversed the trend. That the event made the news at all was more down to the fact that it was witnessed by the winner of the UK version of the television programme Survivor than because it was terribly unusual.

It is still dark when we wake up. We can hear people talking in nearby tents, which must have stirred us.

"Mmmm, that was the best sleep ever", smiles Jen.

"Aw, I feel like I slept for months too", I reply. We lie back and enjoy the feeling of immense relaxation. I hear pots clanking, no doubt breakfast being prepared. The voices we can hear are the usual incoherent babble, just outside the range of understanding exactly what they are saying.

"Noisy bunch", I say, idly, although as we can't understand them they can't be that noisy.

"Porters, I reckon", muses Jen.

"Or other walkers", I say.

"What time do you think it is?"

"Dunno."

"Maybe it's still last night and the voices are people who haven't gone to bed yet", says Jen.

I contemplate the thought. I feel remarkably well slept, which means either that I am or that I'm experiencing a pretty good illusion of being well slept and I'm about to have a very long night of not sleeping. The voices have a sudden laugh together. Maybe what I had assumed to be the sound of breakfast is actually the sound of a drunken celebration.

"I'll check my phone", I say. I sit up to look for the phone and find that my feet are wet.

"Bother, the bottoms of our sleeping bags are soaked!" I say.

Jen sits up. "They've touched the sides and it's rained", she says.

We've had four nights of sleeping in dry high-altitude air and forgotten that, back in the real world of low-altitude, water and camping are not cosy and dry bedfellows.

"It's 5.45am", I say, finding the phone.

"Phew", says Jen, lying back down.

Limu is due to wake us up at six. Last night, he explained that the bureaucracy to leave the park is even slower than entering. Unless we are one of the first groups at the gate, we will spend most of the day sitting around and waiting to be signed out. I can't imagine what can take the time – surely it's just one line of a log that we have to complete – but after just a week in Africa I've learnt to accept the estimates of time (and double them) rather than question their accuracy. If he says we need to be there early, we'll be there early. After 5 days of polè, we're now in a race.

Jen and I use the 15 minutes until six o'clock to partially dry out our sleeping bags and to more gently pack our rucksacks and daypacks. We're first in the breakfast tent for a change. We're told by the waiter that, since we've devoured almost all of the food supplies, we have porridge, tea and eggs on offer for breakfast. Now that we've conquered the mountain, I have no desire to eat any more eggs. With no Milo left, I'm happy to decline the hot drinks as well. That leaves porridge and cold water. There's not even any jam or peanut butter, just some rather odd tasting honey made by bees that live in acacia groves. I try a little and decide the porridge is better plain. For the last 4 days I've eaten everything put in front of me and loved every morsel I've eaten. Now, when I've not even left the mountain, I'm already being fussy with my food. Did the altitude dull my taste-buds and make everything taste great? Maybe it was because I thought that I had to eat everything to get to the top and, now that I don't have to, I'm back to being more selective with what I eat? Or maybe I'm just a pernickety old boot.

"Do you know", says John through a mouthful of plain porridge, "when we reached Stellar Point, if you had all said you'd had enough and were going straight back down, I'd have just followed. I was in sheep mode. You all carried on up the mountain instead, so I just followed. I had no idea what was going on."

"There was no way I was going straight back down without reaching the top", says Jen.

"After the steepness of the scree the last bit after Stellar Point felt like we were going down anyway", I say.

"It took forever for the top to appear though", says Andy. "It felt like about four hours from Stellar to the top."

"No way! I thought it flew by", I say.

"I kept looking for the sign from the guidebook but it just didn't seem to appear", says John. "I thought it took ages too."

"Maybe I just couldn't wait to get there", I wonder.

"I'm not sure how long it felt", says Jen. "I just knew I'd have had to be carried off the mountain before I gave up."

"With all that puking I thought you were going to have to be carried off", I laugh.

"The walking poles were a life-saver", says Andy. "I don't reckon we'd have made it up the scree without them."

John agrees, and Jen and I both nod.

"I'm glad I took three litres of water too, given how much of it froze", I say.

We continue to dissect the walk until breakfast is cleared away around us. We're supposed to leave at seven and, despite what felt like a leisurely breakfast, we're ready in time. Limu joins us at 7.15 and we begin the final three-hour walk to the gate.

The camp is full of activity as we cross to re-enter the forest. We look like we're one of the first to leave. A number of other groups are close to being ready to depart. The South Africans are all kitted up and checking their boots and rucksacks.

"See you at the gate", I smile as we trot past.

"Ya", replies one of the group. He doesn't look too pleased that we're ahead of them again.

"Did you make it?" I shout back, realising that we hadn't seen them since the start of the final ascent.

"Ya, of course", he replies.

"All of you?"

I get an indignant reply. "Ya, ya, all of us, of course."

We disappear into the forest.

Now that we've achieved what we set out to do and the anxiety about whether or not we'll reach the top is over, I don't want to leave. I've enjoyed my time on this mountain so much that I don't really want to rush the last part and leave in a hurry. This is the last time I'll spend here, after all, and most probably I'll never come back. Times like this should be savoured, not gulped down in a probably futile attempt to beat some dire African administration. As we walk down at pace into the increasingly dense forest I wonder whether to hang back a little, but a greater urge overtakes me. I don't want to lose the race to the gate. There's no official race going on, there's every reason to stay and enjoy our last few minutes in one of the most beautiful places on Earth, and no prize for getting there first. Except that I don't really want to see the South Africans lumber past us with their smug grins and we-beat-you-in-the-end looks. Or the French bloke who leaves women for dead. And for some reason it would feel quite good to be the first down. Where does the competitiveness come from? I almost forget that it would be great not to wait for ages with the administration. We trot on.

Behind us we can occasionally hear the sound of voices. There's possibly a French intonation to the accent. We press on.

I'm clearly not the only one of us who doesn't want to be overtaken. None of us is openly rushing but no-one is hanging around either. The more we descend into the cloud-forest, the more muddy and slippery the path becomes. My gaiters are hanging off my day-pack, as I took the decision that we'd not need them today. Consequently my trousers are covered in mud splatters up to my knees. I could stop and put on the gaiters, something that involves removing my boots and at least a two-minute stop. Then again, I'll be putting my trousers into the laundry in Moshi regardless. I don't stop.

Although we are descending at a reasonable pace, the porters are haring past us. I spot Jen's rucksack whizz past on one porter's back and quickly take a picture. When I later look at the picture I notice that he's also carrying my rucksack on his head. With 24Kg on his back and head, he still runs past us on a slippery path. My respect for these men increases yet again.

After just two hours and twenty minutes and with a slight drizzle beginning to fall, we arrive at Mweka Gate, 1,900m. We're the second group down, beaten by a pair of Italians who are signing for their green certificates. Green certificates?

"Green certificates", explains Limu, "are for reaching Stellar Point only. Gold certificates are for reaching Uhuru Peak."

Well that's all right then – we're the first down of the people who made it to the top. The French pair arrives a few minutes after us. It's the same leave-them-for-dead man I spoke to on my way down from the summit yesterday, together with a much older man.

"Hello", I smile.

"Hi"

I'm not sure what to say next. "Just the two of you?" I try.

"Yes, this is my father," he replies.

"Ah", I nod, then realise that I didn't see the father yesterday. "Did you make it to the top too?" I ask him.

The father looks at his son.

"My father's 69, he doesn't speak English", says the son, as if his father's age explained his lack of mastery of the English language. "Yes, we both made it. My father got there at 7.30."

I'm speechless. Not only did he leave a woman fainting in his race to be first to the top, he also left his 69-year old father to make his own way. Clearly he must also have passed his father on the way down. What on earth could he have said? "Come on dad, you can do it … see you at breakfast"?

The son is happily oblivious to my amazement and we are fortunately interrupted by reaching the front of the queue to sign out, the Italians having finally received their certificates, signed the log book and moved off. For a moment the Frenchman looks like he is about to attempt an outrageous manoeuvre to jump the queue. He's foiled by John "accidentally" dropping a walking pole in front of him.

The signing-out takes place outside a wooden hut. Again there is no gate for us to walk symbolically through. Somehow it takes half an hour to wade through four lines of text (one for each of our details) and eight signatures (two each, one from the gate-keeper and one from Limu). A mix up with signatures and details almost puts the French in front of us again, only this time some frantic shouting by me saves the day. Well, I wasn't about to let the ultra-competitive French get in first, was I?

The French and the Italians chat in broken English about the football. Both teams were in the semi-finals and it appears that both have won through to the final. (One more reason to hold our ground, then.) If we were in London then the World Cup would be the main topic of conversation. It all seems such a long way away, both in distance and in importance. I wonder if that would have been the case had England won that night in Moshi.

We walk back up to the Mweka Gate sign for a set of pictures of the four of us leaving the park. One of the South Africans is washing his feet in the water-channel alongside the path.

"It feels great", he shouts. It does look good and I'm tempted. Maybe after the pictures.

"Well done for making it to the top?" asks Andy.

"Oh ya", says the South African, as if it was never in question. "We all got there. Amazing experience. You guys beat us though. Respect."

Limu arrives. "No, no wash feet there! Drinking water for village!"

The South African eases himself out of the water, shrugs and puts his boots on. We gather Limu into the pictures and ask Patrick, who has also arrived, to take the pictures. Each picture he takes is accompanied by an exaggerated pressing of his finger, making the whole camera drop an inch on one side. I haven't the heart to correct him after all his mostly silent and often un-noticed help over the last few days. The blur will add to the character of the pictures. Sure enough, the pictures are blurred when I check them.

"Let's go", says Limu to his heroes for the last time..

The mini-bus will meet us lower down the path. We walk past the signing-out hut. There is a queue of three or four groups waiting to sign out. At the rate we went through, there's already a few hours work there. In contrast to Umbwe, all along the path people are trying to sell us ornamental knives, banana-leaf pictures, bead necklaces and other undoubtedly authentic trinkets. I'm tempted to tell them to go to Umbwe and sell Snickers bars instead. John stops to check out what they're selling. Jen feels a little threatened so we walk ahead with Limu, who just ignores all of them. Two girls balancing packs on their heads walk slowly up the road towards us. I consider taking their picture but can't bring myself to so blatantly photograph them. As they pass, they say something to each other. Limu laughs.

"What did they say?" I ask.

"One girl said 'Something's wrong with us. They didn't take our picture.' The other girl said 'Good!'"

The van arrives and takes us back to our hotel in Moshi. As we leave the minibus in the hotel forecourt, John is accosted by a local trying to sell him something. The rest of us scoot inside and leave him to it. The receptionist, a tall, well-built lady in a maroon uniform, is writing a list in a ledger. She completes her entry before looking up at us.

"Hi", says Jen. "We stayed here a few days ago. We've just climbed the mountain and want to check back in for tonight, collect our stuff we left with you …"

The receptionist stops her continuing by calling in Swahili to the room behind her, from where another woman in a maroon uniform emerges. She has the air of a manager called away from important managerial duties. She ignores Jen and raises her head to me in a gesture that says "Yes?".

Jen, not one to be ignored, repeats herself.

The manager looks at her, then me, and then calls out to two men who I hadn't noticed standing behind us at the rear of the lobby. They hurry forwards and follow the manager into a back room. They re-appear quickly with some of our bags, which they deposit on the floor of the lobby. Jen and I pick out ours as the porters go back and return with some more. Andy finds his and John's. There are still some spare bags on the floor when the porters return for a third time with even more bags.

"I've got all our bags", says Andy to Jen and me.

"Us too", I say.

"We've got all our bags", says Andy to the men.

The manager shouts at the men, who stop mid-step like burglars caught in the torchlight in an early Hollywood film. The manager shouts again and they hurry back with the spare bags.

"We've also got some things in the safe", I say, handing her our receipt that I've recovered from my bag. The manager takes the receipt and walks back into her office.

"I bet the fat-boy's got ours", says Andy, searching through his rucksack. "What's he up to out there?"

The hotel porters re-appear and start to pick up the bags.

"No, no," says Andy, waving his hands at the porters.

"We carry", says one of the porters, carrying on picking up the bags.

"No!" snaps Andy. "We can carry our own bags, thanks."

Caught in another Hollywood comedy moment, the second porter turns to me for support. I shake my head, also happy to carry my own bags for the first time in a week. Both the porters unload and wander off, looking back both surprised and crestfallen as they go. I look at our bags and can share their surprise – there's a lot of stuff here.

"Aha," smiles Andy, oblivious to the offence he's just caused and producing a damp and screwed-up pink receipt.

The manager returns with our envelope, opens it, counts out our money and checks all the other valuables off the list. She takes Andy's receipt and quickly returns with his envelope.

"Right, that's it, showers here we come", says Jen.

"What about the laundry?" asks Andy, gathering the last of his valuables from the reception desk.

"Good call", I say.

Andy looks up to ask the manager but she's already returned to her office. He turns to the receptionist instead.

"Can we still get our laundry done and returned to us by the morning before our bus leaves?" he asks her. She shrugs and calls in Swahili to the room behind her. The manager re-appears and this time cocks her head at Andy.

"We want to have our clothes laundered and returned by the morning before our bus leaves", he says. "Is that OK?"

The manager looks at the clock behind her and turns back to us with a familiar doubtful expression.

"You need to see the head housemaid", she replies, speaking to us for the first time and in excellent English. She turns and heads back to her office, no doubt to continue the important managerial duties that we had once again interrupted.

"Where is she?" I call to the rapidly retreating back.

The manager returns to the desk. "She will be upstairs, cleaning in one of the rooms", she says. "If you walk along the corridor and check the bedrooms you will find her."

"OK, thank you", I reply.

This time there is no rush to complete unknown duties. She stands silently and watches us load up with our various mounds of belongings. It feels like she is waiting for something although I can't think what on earth that might be. Then I notice that Limu has arrived behind us. The attentiveness is clearly for his benefit.

"I will see you in the bar", he says.

"OK, no worries", says Andy, who is struggling to pick up all his bags and try and gather John's as well. He turns to Jen. "Where's the fat boy?"

"For the award ceremony", Limu continues.

Jen giggles. I look at Limu and he is deadly serious.

"Awards ceremony?" asks Andy

"I'll be in the bar", Limu nods, "with Patrick."

"Right, we'll, er, see you in the bar then", says Andy, looking at us incredulously from underneath an enormous pile of bags. "Bugger it", he continues, and gives up trying to pick up John's bags. "He can bring them himself."

Limu waves at the manager, who smiles back and returns to her back-room duties. As he leaves, Limu looks at our bags and grins. For the first time in a week, we have to carry all our belongings – the daypacks, rucksacks, bin-bags of extras left in the hotel and the valuables from the hotel safe. It's a bit of a shock after days of porters helping and we stagger up the stairs, belongings dripping from each arm, tucked under each armpit and balanced in front of our faces. There is washing hanging on the lines outside that I hope is a good omen that our laundry can still be done. After a titanic struggle to fit our key in the lock without dropping anything, Jen and I explode into our room and scatter everything across the floor and beds. I ignore the mess and head straight back out of the room and along the corridor to find the head housekeeper.

"Ooh, stop!" shouts Jen after me. "Look at the mud everywhere."

I stop and look down at the clumps of mud I'm trailing behind me across an obviously just-cleaned floor.

"Oops", I say, looking around to see if I've been spotted.

A porter is carrying a pile of bags up the stairs, followed by a smiling John.

"Ah," John grins. "What you need is your boots cleaned for $3! I've just given mine to the bloke who was hassling me outside and I'll have them back within the hour."

"You'll never see them again", laughs Jen.

A look of uncertainty crosses his face. "No, I will", says John, seriously. "He's one of the hotel staff. Well, he was in the hotel grounds."

"If your boots come back clean then I'll consider it. $3 is pretty good given the state of these fellers", I say, looking at the mess all around me.

"Which is our room?" asks John

"Next door", I point. "Andy's in there already."

The porter goes straight in. John follows as I tread carefully back to our bedroom and take off my very muddy boots. Jen does the same and, by the time we re-emerge, Andy is walking back down the corridor with a chambermaid who turns out to be the head housekeeper.

"Yes", she says. "If you give us your laundry now we will wash it for you."

"And she says it will dry by the morning", confirms Andy.

The head housekeeper looks less certain. She waggles her hand.

"Maybe mostly dry?" she says, looking to see if we are happy with that.

"That's alright, although there is quite a lot", checks Jen.

"When will we get the laundry?" asked the head housekeeper.

"In, say, half an hour?" says Jen, hopefully.

The head housekeeper nods agreement.

"Where shall we bring it?" asks Andy.

"Here", says the head housekeeper. "I will be here." She looks at the floor.

"Ah, if you give me a mop ...", I begin.

The head housekeeper looks both shocked and amused. "No, no, if you give me your boots we can clean them too. One dollar."

"One dollar?!" John has come out of his door to catch the end of the conversation. "I just paid three dollars to the bloke outside!"

"You're an idiot, fat-boy", says Andy.

John looks as if he is about to rise to the bait but calms himself. "Ah, it's only $2. Mine will be cleaner than yours."

"OK boys, let's move", says Jen. "Limu and Patrick are waiting. There's an awards ceremony to be had!"

We find our guides sitting outside the bar with a bottle each, next to the swimming pool where we first met Limu for our introductory talk. The receptionist was still filling in her ledger as we passed and didn't even look up. Once again, Kilimanjaro is covered by clouds instead of providing a fitting backdrop to our finale.

"A celebratory drink?" asks John.

"I think it's Kili time!" says Jen with a cheer.

"Same for me", I add.

"And me, fat-boy", says Andy.

"You can help me carry them, then", says John to Andy.

"You can carry four bottles on your own", says Andy, in mock derision, and sits down.

John ignores him. "And what are you drinking?" he asks Limu and Patrick. He peers at their bottles. "Ginger ale? Can I get you a proper drink?"

"We are not allowed to drink on duty", says Limu. He looks at Patrick a little sheepishly.

"Go on, you've finished now", says Jen, egging them on.

Limu shakes his head. "We are not allowed", he repeats.

"No-one will know", says Andy. "John's paying too."

Limu continues to look a little sheepish. "OK, another ginger ale." Patrick nods in agreement.

"With something in it?" suggests John with a grin.

Limu pauses.

"Double Bacardi", he says. Patrick nods again.

"Hey, you sneaky boys", grins Jen. "Is there one in there already?"

Limu looks even more sheepish and grins.

John is about to go to the bar when the barmaid walks out with her notepad ready to take our order.

"Ah", says John. "We'll have four Kilis …" He extends his hand to Limu to order his own drink. Limu remains silent, so John continues for him. "… and two ginger ales and double Bacardis."

"Double?" asks the barmaid.

"Yes", nods Limu.

"And who will pay?" she asks him, sternly.

"We'll pay", says John, and Jen confirms we'll split the bill.

The barmaid sighs. "OK", she says in a resigned voice that included an unspoken "I think you are stupid paying for drinks for these idiots but on your head be it."

When the barmaid returns with our drinks, Limu sets about the awards ceremony with all the formality of the queen conveying a knighthood. All smiles and sheepishness have disappeared and his tone becomes solemn. He stands at the head of the table with the four certificates laid out in front of him and then, for each of us, he reads out the inscription, shakes our hand and waits while the other three each take a photo.

"This is to certify", says Limu, "that Mr. Andrew Leighton has *successfully* climbed Mount Kilimanjaro, the highest peak in Africa, right to the summit, Uhuru Peak, five-thousand, eight-hundred and ninety-five metres."

Andy is followed by John, me and then Jen. We get more and more into the swing of it with each person that goes up. The stifled giggles for Andy are applause and a rousing cheer by the time Jen is presented with her certificate. Limu is smiling again, obviously pleased with our enthusiasm.

With the formality over, we settle back to enjoy our Kilis and properly relax for the first time in days. Only there is no relaxation. Limu and Patrick both look a little shifty now and the conversation is awkward. What are their plans now? A shrug. When will they next climb the mountain? Another shrug. Was it easy for them? OK. All our questions are answered politely but without enthusiasm. It is as if they are expecting something else …

"Oh, shit!" I whisper to Jen as the light dawns. "They're waiting for a tip."

"Oh yeah!"

"How much though?"

"Dunno", she replies. I too am genuinely unsure what is acceptable. On the Inca trail, tipping was organised very systematically by our tour leader. He knew exactly how many porters, cooks and guides we had, suggested an appropriate amount for each of them, added up the total and divided it by the number of walkers. After some splitting up of a number of the larger notes to make each pile add up for each porter/cook/guide, we then wondered how and when to give it to them. We were told that they wanted to sing for us and it was a great opportunity for us to give them the tip. What a happy coincidence. 28 of us squeezed in on one side of the long dining table and the porters tramped in and stood on the other and sang us a few traditional songs while clapping their hands. Neither they nor us knew where to look, so excruciating and staged for tipping was the situation. It all ended with each of them being handed a wad of dollars before they disappeared into the night and we were all grateful the embarrassing transaction was over. Asking the tour leader later, we were assured that this was the only way to ensure that the chief guide didn't pocket most or even the entire tip and leave little or nothing for everyone else. An eminently honest plan and probably worth the dreadful singing.

Sitting here in Moshi, we've clearly missed the opportunity to ensure that everyone gets a share of any tip we give. The three batteries we gave to our nameless waiter suddenly seem a little tight-fisted. I nudge Andy.

"We need to tip them", I whisper.

"Yeah, I know", he whispers back having caught on to the situation. "How much?"

I giggle. "That's what I asked. I was hoping you'd have an idea."

Andy turns to John, who shrugs. Andy turns back to me and shrugs too. It's an awkward situation. Jen and I don't know Andy and John well enough to know how much they'd think is an acceptable tip. So far we've not really spent any money together, other than a meal at this hotel before the climb when we really had no choice but to eat here. We've nothing to guide us as to whether they are well-off professionals or still paying off their student loans. I'm reluctant to suggest an amount that's too much and put them in an awkward situation, and I'm also wary of suggesting too little and appearing mean.

"We could ask them how much is usual or acceptable", I suggest doubtfully. "I know it sounds bonkers but I couldn't say whether we're talking $50 or $150."

John shrugs again and mouths "OK".

I look at Jen and she shrugs and nods in agreement. Everyone is looking at me, the originator of the splendid idea. Bother.

"Erm", I begin. Limu and Patrick look up expectantly. "We'd like to give you a tip." They nod gravely. I press on. "What would be an acceptable amount? I mean, what is a normal tip?" They look back at me silently. I flounder and, rather than stop and wait for a response, flounder on. "We want to give something to all the porters and the chef and the waiter." They nod even more gravely, look at each other and nod some more. "You will make sure that they get some of the tip?" They nod again. This time I've run out of things to say.

Limu speaks, finally, thank goodness. "Oh yes, we share the tip. We will make sure all porters will get a tip."

We look at each other, waiting for the other to speak. I feel like I'd have a better chance if this was a deal for a trinket in a market, rather than in this perverse and reverse negotiation. It's supposed to be us deciding how good the service has been on the trip and giving an appropriate token of our appreciation, not them deciding how good they think their service was. My good idea is starting to feel rather uncomfortable. Inevitably, I break first.

"So, what tip do you normally receive?"

Limu squirms. Aha, I've got him! I stop floundering and wait for him to continue.

"Well, maybe … maybe … I don't know … $200 each?" he suggests.

Yikes. This was just beyond the top end of what I was expecting and a quick look at the boys reveals that it's the same for them. From the four of us combined that's $800. That's a lot of money in London – my month's rent, for example. In Moshi you must be able to found a small dynasty upon it.

"Maybe $150, maybe $200?" continues Limu, aware that he's 'maybe' pushed the boundary a little far.

So what do we, the sophisticated, worldly-wise Westerners do? We can't haggle, that's for sure, and we can't easily talk amongst ourselves when our tippees are patiently listening to every word. We all look at each other, shrugging and not speaking. For the second time in barely a minute I'm hoping someone else will speak first. This time I'm determined it's not me.

Limu and Patrick pretend to talk amongst themselves. Our silent game of shrug tennis is thankfully ended by Jen, who says, firmly "I think they're worth it. Let's pay them." A pause.

"I agree", chips in Andy.

"$150 or $200?" I check.

"I don't care", says John, in a "get me out of this situation as fast as possible" voice.

"How much is that?" asks Jen.

"$150 is about £90, $200 is about £120", I say.

"It's only £30 difference", says Andy, "whether we pay $150 or $200."

"Let's just pay $200", argues Jen. "There are all the porters too, and it's not much difference."

While I muse over whether any of the porters, waiter or chef will ever see any of the money, John has had enough. "Let's do it", he says.

"OK", says Andy.

They all look at me for my final agreement. "Done", I say quickly. There is no way I am going to prolong the excruciation any longer. We collect our respective $200, Andy lending John some as he didn't bring enough to the bar, and hand it over to Limu and Patrick with many thank-yous and handshakes. Limu accepts it graciously and puts it in his pocket, to be counted and divided later.

"I want a shower", says Jen, finishing her Kili and easily returning the situation to normality.

"We need to get our clothes into the laundry too", I add.

"Fancy heading into town this afternoon?" asks Andy.

"Sure", says Jen. She lowers her voice. "Shall we ask these two if they want to join us for a drink in the bar this evening?"

"Yeah, good idea", says Andy.

Jen turns to the guides and extends our offer. They are pleased to be invited and a little reluctant.

"I give you my cell number. You can beep me later?" suggest

Limu.

Jen laughs. "What's beep? Is that a text or a call?"

Limu taps his phone keypad with his thumb, miming sending a text.

"I'll beep you!" giggles Jen. They swap numbers while we boys finish our Kilis (yes, Jen did finish her Kili before us). Another round of thank-yous and handshakes follows as we leave our guides to finish their undercover alcopops. As we walk back to our rooms, we agree to meet the boys in an hour for a walk into town.

"I think $200 was an OK tip", says Jen.

"It's a lot of money around here", says John.

"It's fine. I think Limu did make a difference as to whether we all got to the top or not", I add.

"True, they were good boys. I'm happy with that", says Andy.

"Heroes", says John.

Our room smells of damp and sweaty clothes, probably rivalled in intensity only by us. We tip-toe our way around the festering piles.

"Right, let's get the washing into a bag and give it to the cleaner", says Jen, rather more chirpily than I'm feeling as I survey the festering scene. There are clothes crawling out of every bag. "Where are our spare bin bags?"

"Wait, there's bound to be one of those little lists around here somewhere", I say.

"A?"

"Here it is", I say, finding it under the ashtray next to the television with a white plastic bag attached to it.

"Oh, cool, they give us a bag to put the washing in", says Jen, full of enthusiasm again. She gathers up one of the steaming piles. "Let's fill it up."

"We have to itemise it all first", I say, looking gloomily at the list.

"A?" repeats Jen, grabbing the list from me. She skims down it, her enthusiasm dwindling. "Oh, bugger, that'll take ages. Does it matter?"

"It does if you want all your clothes back", I say. "Anyway, everything is charged at different rates, so we need to work out how much it will cost."

Jen laughs. "Hee, you can get your 'long casual slacks' cleaned", she says.

"Cool, I'll put them both in for a wash", I reply. I take the list back and look for another ridiculously dated description. "You can wash your safari suits if you like", I suggest.

"Dry clean only, they won't be back in time", replies Jen, peering at the list again. "How about your flannels?"

"I'll need them in the shower. Kitenge suit?"

"My what?"

"I dunno either."

"Shall we just get on with it?"

"OK", I say, noticing that the two most expensive items on the list are "Dress – pleated" for a woman and "3 Pc suite" for a man. I wonder if the porters carry the suite for travellers requiring just that little bit more comfort. Maybe the sofa extends out into a bed – much more comfortable than a roll-mat. Then again, if someone can afford to have a three piece suite carried up the mountain, they can probably afford a decent bed as well.

Jen's enthusiasm returns and we quickly marshal our clothes into similar piles before deliberating over which category we place our long johns (eventually deciding on "Under Pant") and woollen gloves (nothing close, so we take them back out).

"Do you reckon they'll be able to do all this by the morning?" asks Jen, looking doubtfully at the enormous bag.

"I'm more concerned for the poor woman who will no doubt be doing this all by hand", I reply.

The cleaner is waiting outside when we open our door. She smiles and takes the bag and list.

"Is that OK?" asks Jen.

"Yes, thank you", nods the cleaner, still smiling. She seems genuinely pleased to see so much dirty washing. We are genuinely pleased to see the back of it.

John and Andy's door opens and a similar sized bag appears in Andy's arms.

"Thank you, thank you", smiles the cleaner to him.

"Thank *you!*" he says back.

There is a moment's hesitation as we all stand looking at each other. The cleaner is waiting for us to say something else or go back to our rooms. We return to our rooms. I'm not sure I'll ever get used to this master and servant thing.

I'm a reluctant shaver normally, seeing it as a routine necessity rather than a daily pick-me-up. Normally, that is, except when it's been a few days and the going's been a bit dirty. A shave followed by a hot shower and clean clothes is just the most fabulous feeling when you've not had any of them for a week. We've been waiting for this moment since we left camp this morning and the delays for the awards ceremony and laundry have only increased the anticipation.

Jen turns on the shower as I begin to run some water for the shave. The shower dribbles out.

"This is not going to be funny", she says.

I turn off the tap to the sink and the shower spurts into life. We both sigh with relief.

The sink has no plug so I have to block the plughole with toilet paper. I quickly run the water while Jen collects her gels and shampoos. The toilet paper appears to hold back most of the water but starts to disintegrate as I swish my razor around. My strategy is to fill the bowl as full as possible and swish the razor as little possible. I manage half a shave before the water runs so low that the pieces of paper clog my razor. I scoop out the gloop, throw it down the loo and make another plug with some more paper.

"Er, Jen", I say. "Be careful for a few seconds."

"What's that?" she calls.

I turn on the tap and the powerful, steaming shower becomes a freezing dribble.

"Yikes!" shouts Jen. "What's happened?"

"My water ran out. I won't be long."

"Brrrrrrr", says Jen, wrapping her arms around herself.

The volume of water coming out of the tap bears no resemblance to the volume that was coming out of the shower a few moments ago, and the sink takes quite a while to fill. Jen is stamping her feet by the time I turn off the tap.

"Aaargh!", she screams, as the water sprays out of the shower.

"Shit, are you OK?" I dash over to the shower, expecting her to be burnt.

"Aw, that was FREEZING!"

"Oops, sorry." I stick my head into the shower to give Jen an apologetic kiss and get a soapy nose instead.

"Have you found your wallet?" asks Jen, drying her hair with her towel.

"Shit, no!" I say. "I'd forgotten all about it."

I haven't given it another thought since we left the hotel six days ago. At home, I always have my wallet and phone to hand or at least know exactly where both are at all times. With nowhere to spend money, I've completely forgotten the missing wallet. Even when paying the tip I just took the money from the clear plastic bag I'd left in the safe.

I check all my bags and pockets, twice, and don't find it.

"Bother", I proclaim. "That's going to be a pain."

"You should check again with the hotel", says Jen.

"Hmmm." I'm not hopeful. In addition to the inconvenience, the wallet came from a trip I made to Montreal a few years and I'm quite attached to it. It also contains my London Underground travelcard photograph that I'm quite fond of. Not because I look good in it. Far from it. I took it in an automatic booth in Tooting Bec on the day before I started work for the first time, and it's amusing for my fantastically long bouffant-style hair that I'd actually just had cut so that I looked smart on my first day.

I trudge downstairs to reception, past the smirking giraffes, to find the receptionist still completing her ledger entries. She looks up at me.

"Er, I don't suppose anyone has handed in a wallet, have they?" I ask.

She shrugs and calls in Swahili to the room behind her. I'm beginning to understand how Bill Murray felt in Groundhog Day. The manager re-appears.

"I was wondering if you had had a wallet handed in?" I repeated.

The manager shakes her head slightly.

"Maybe a few days ago?" I continue. "I think I left it in the restaurant."

"I will check for you", says the manager. She turns and heads into her office, returning barely five seconds later with my wallet in her hands.

"That's it!" I exclaim.

"It was found in the restaurant", says the manager. No kidding. I open it and find that the cards are present but the money is missing. Thankfully all I had in it was our remaining Kenyan shillings and about £50 in English notes. A significant loss, for sure, but not compared to all the dollars we've got with us or the hassle of cancelling all my cards and continuing the holiday without them.

"It is yours?" she asks, watching me check it.

"Yes. The money's missing but all the cards are here", I explain.

The manager looks offended. "There is money missing? Are you sure?"

"Yes, the wallet is empty. I had maybe $100 in here before. It's not important though. I'm happy to get the wallet back."

"I will check with the kitchen staff. There shouldn't be anything missing. I will let you know", she says sternly.

"No really, it's not important", I repeat. The chances of getting my cash back are non-existent.

"I will check", she repeats.

Jen, John and Andy appear, walking down the stairs.

"You've got it, yay", cheers Jen.

"Yeah, pretty lucky", I reply, still pleased at having the wallet returned.

"Is it all there?" she asks.

"All the cards but no cash – only about $100 missing, I reckon."

"That's not good", says Jen with a frown.

"I will check and let you know", repeats the manager, maintaining her stern-ness for the benefit of the new arrivals.

"That's quite a lot to lose", says Andy, "and you'll have to cancel the cards too."

I hadn't thought of that and for a moment the jubilation fades. He's right, that's exactly what I should do. Yet here they are in my hands, looking to the entire world as if they haven't been touched. And they probably haven't been used either.

"I think I'll risk it until I can check my balance", I say, hoping to convince myself.

"Really?" says Andy in a surprised tone. He's not helping.

"Aw, it'll be fine", says Jen. That's better.

"I'll check my balance in town. I reckon they've not been touched", I say, firmly. Rapidly changing the subject before any more comments sway my mind, I say "Anyway, does everyone feel great? Clean shave, steaming shower, clean clothes, ah."

"Pretty good", says John. "Pretty good."

"The shower was a bit pants", says Andy.

"It was alright", says John. "Stop moaning."

"I'm just saying", says Andy, "that it wasn't the best. I'd just get it the right temperature and the water disappeared, then the pressure came back and the temperature went all over the place."

"Well it was alright when I had mine", says John.

"I reckon there was someone running water somewhere in the hotel at the same time", says Andy. "What was your's like?"

Jen and I look at each other, knowing it was probably us. "Er, fine", I say. "Hot and powerful." Jen looks about to continue but John cuts in.

"Just like mine", he says. "Stop moaning."

"I'm not moaning, fat boy. They asked how the shower was."

"Shall we go to town and celebrate?" I interrupt.

Outside the sun is shining through hazy cloud-cover. It is comfortably warm. We walk the mile into town and enjoy the feeling of walking at a normal speed with clean clothes. We change some money at the bank and try to find a bar where we can sit outside and have a drink. We wander around the bustling town for a while with no luck. The wide and unpaved roads are full of battered cars and chattering people. The town hasn't succumbed to tourists at all, with most if not all shops catering for the local trade. The streets are lined with shabby stalls selling brash clothes and second hand shoes. Many of the stalls are simply blankets laid over the pavement with the goods arranged haphazardly around a seller sitting in the middle. Authentic African stalls in Moshi sell cheap Western tat to wannabe-Western Africans while the "authentic" African stalls on the road to Moshi sell expensive African tat to wannabe-ethnic Westerners.

We eventually find a tree-shaded, outside bar but it only serves soft drinks. It should also have a great view of Kili but once again the mountain is covered by cloud. We really are destined never to see it from ground level.

We stay for a coke and decide that if our celebrations are going to happen, then they're going to have to happen at the hotel. We walk back and head straight for the bar. It's 4pm and we order our second round of bottles of Kilimanjaro of the day. The bar is empty, so we sit outside by the pool.

"Hey, look, mine was born yesterday", says John. He points to his label where, just like on a bottle of Budweiser, it says the date on which the bottle was filled. Sure enough, it has yesterday's date, brewed in Dar es Salaam, some 300 miles away.

Within a few minutes, a group of ten Irish join us with beers in their hands. They look as unshaven and unwashed as we did a few hours ago.

One of them calls over to us. "Are you guys going up Kili?"

We all laugh, much to his bemusement.

"Ah, it's not your thing, right?" he tries.

"No, we got back at lunchtime", says John, recovering first.

We join them, taking some group photos of them and sharing mountain stories. They've come down the Marangu Route, which sounds much longer than ours. They hit camp at 7pm last night and took seven hours to reach the gate today. All except two of them made it to the top, and the two seemed pleased to have reached Gilman's Point. Jen looks like she can't quite comprehend this but doesn't press the point.

As the Irish drift off one-by-one to clean up, Jen beeps Limu to join us for dinner. He arrives within fifteen minutes. He's hiding it well but he's clearly had a fair few drinks this afternoon. Hopefully he's been celebrating another successful trip rather than the generosity of our tip. We buy him dinner.

We talk about the walk, then the conversation turns to his life in Moshi.

"Where is Mrs. Limu this evening?" asks Jen.

Limu is rather coy.

"Oooh", we tease. "Tell us. Where is she tonight? Will she come out to meet us?"

"No, no", Limu shakes his head.

"Oh, go on, what's her number?" asks Jen. "I'll beep her!"

We tease him and grill him relentlessly and he looks coyer and coyer. Finally he cracks.

"She's over there", he says, pointing to a table across the bar where a local woman has been sat for the last ten minutes.

"No way!" I say.

"Hey, Mrs. Limu", shouts Jen. "Come over here and join us!"

Mrs. Limu – we are never told her real name – joins us. She's rather shy with us, although I suspect that in the privacy of home she is much more commanding. She doesn't speak very good English, so all our questions at her are directed through Limu.

"Has she been up Kili?" asks John.

"No", replies Limu, "she is a bit chunky."

John laughs. "No!" I cry.

"She is oh-bees", continues Limu, matter-of-factly. "Oh-bees."

Mrs. Limu shakes her head. She may not have good English but some things she clearly understands. She looks like she's heard it all before. She's not slim, for sure, but obese is a little harsh.

Dinner arrives. Although we offer to buy Mrs. Limu some food, Limu answers "no" for her before eating his huge burger and chips. Jen makes sure that Mrs. Limu shares her food, which draws annoyed glances from Limu.

Limu's sister arrives in the same manner as Mrs. Limu, via a separate table until she is noticed and brought into the fold. She appears to be good friends with Mrs. Limu and she speaks the best English of the three of them, so interprets a lot of the conversation. She looks about mid-twenties in age and is similar in size and shape to Mrs. Limu. It quickly becomes apparent that Limu's sister is in the market for a husband. Thankfully I am clearly with Jen and am immediately off the market. John makes it known that he has a girlfriend and so the attention shifts to Andy, who moves uneasily in his seat.

"Would you marry Andy?" John asks, mischievously.

Limu's sister nods and looks shyly at Andy.

"He snores, you know", says John.

She smiles.

"John ...", warns Andy.

"Would you move to England?" I ask.

"Do you want his address?" says John.

Suddenly overcoming her shyness and sensing an opportunity, Limu's sister blurts out "Where do you live?".

"Er, Leeds, no, Halifax", says Andy.

"What is your address?" she persists.

John nearly falls of his chair trying to hide his laughter.

"It's a village near Halifax", lies Andy.

"What religion are you", she continues.

The change of tack momentarily stumps Andy.

"What are you?" he replies.

"Catholic."

"I'm protestant!" He is too, although he'd be Jewish if that helped right now.

Limu's sister looks dejected. This appears to be a major sticking point.

"You can convert to Catholicism", tries John, in a desperate hope to keep the pressure on Andy.

"No way", says Andy, never more resolute in his faith.

Limu's sister senses the opportunity is lost and turns to talk to Mrs. Limu, and so the holiday romance ends as quickly as it began.

As I start to wonder how many more of the Limu clan are going to join us, they announce that they are leaving. Limu can barely stand and seems very happy. Mrs. Limu has a "wait till I get you home" look. We all hug and shake hands and then they are gone.

The evening is cooler, so we move inside to find the Irish standing at the bar singing folk songs. They are each singing a song in turn, solo, and they are scarily good. Whoever takes the floor just stands there and belts out a tune, word and note perfect. They ask us to join in and, if we don't take a physical step backwards then we've definitely taken a fair few mental ones.

"Ah, go orn, sing us a song", says one of them, a twenty-something who has just sung Danny Boy better than I've ever heard it sung.

"Not a chance, we don't know any songs", John replies, laughing.

"Yer muss know wun sorng", says another. "Here, how abou' tiss." He takes a sip from his drink.

"Well, I'm rumblin' in this JCB …"

Now, do you know anyone who knows all the lyrics of The JCB Song? No, nor me. Yet this man stood there and sang the entire thing, from start to finish, better than Nizlopi.

" … I'm Luke, I'm five, and my dad's Bruce Lee. Drives me round in his JCB." He stops and takes another sip of his drink. Everyone cheers and claps.

"Now it's yur turn", he says, waving his hand in our direction. "Yer muss know wun sorng."

"Nope", says John, firmly shaking his head.

"I could get my iPod. Maybe we can find one song we know some of the lyrics to", I suggest.

"You could go to the bar", suggests Jen.

"Good point. Four fresh Kilis coming up."

"Maybe yer know the chorus to someting", suggests one of the older singers.

"Nope", laughs John. "We're English. We're brought up to go to the pub and drink beer, not sing songs. Well, unless England are playing, of course."

I consider pointing out that I'm not English and decide that saying I'm Welsh is not a smart move. If Wales is a nation of male voice choirs, I'm the one who carries the hymn sheets.

"There yer go, Swing Low!" he replies.

"Nope", John shakes his head.

"We don't know the words!" cries Jen.

Another singer starts up with what sounds like a subtle and good-humoured anti-English hymn. I buy the drinks and carry them over to a table on the other side of the bar. The others come over and join me. We try and think of any song where we know even a vaguely creditable section.

"The Portuguese beat us in here last week, this week it's the turn of the Irish", says Andy. "I give up."

"Ah, but we all beat the mountain", smiles Jen.

"To Kili", says John, raising his glass.

"To Kili!", we all cheer.

"To bed", says Jen. "It's one o'clock and I'm pissed."

AFTERWORD

Our bus the next day for the second leg of our trip is almost identical to the one from Nairobi in which we crossed the border. Identical except for the addition of a sign at the front of the bus that reads as follows.

CAUTION
BEWARE OF CONMEN AT THE NAMANGA BORDER
IMPALA SHUTTLE DOES NOT HAVE AN AGENT AT
NAMANGA
IN CASE OF A PROBLEM PLEASE CONTACT OUR DRIVER.
ANY MONEY TRANSACTION AT THE BOARDER
WILL BE AT YOUR OWN RISK

MANAGEMENT
IMPALA SHUTTLE

Now wouldn't that have been handy on the bus when we actually crossed the Namanga border?

We drive away from Moshi towards Arusha. I stare out of the bus at the sunny scene and marvel that Kili is still locked in the clouds. I feel unlucky not to have seen Kili in all our time at ground level but I'm thankful that the weather at the top was near-perfect.

Suddenly I notice a shiny-white peak sticking out above the

clouds, much higher above the horizon than I'd been looking.

"Look, Kili!" I shout excitedly.

Most people in the bus peer over and try to see, some standing up to get a better view. Everyone does what I'd been doing, which was to look too low above the horizon.

"Nah, it's just a cloud", dismisses one of the other passengers and sits back down.

"No, look higher", I say and point upwards.

Everyone's necks simultaneously stretch a few inches upwards and there is a collective "Woooow!"

That is a seriously tall mountain to climb. And we climbed it.

– The End –

SO WHAT DID MAKE A DIFFERENCE TO GETTING TO THE TOP?

Before leaving the UK, we read a lot of books and internet sites and listened to a lot of people with a lot of theories, but what was the truth and what was fiction? What were simply old wives tales and urban myths? What do you need to buy before you go? And what really made a difference to getting to the top?

Urban Myth or Sound Advice?

Let's start with the biggest one – **"altitude sickness strikes both the fit and the fat."** This does appear to be true. In our group, which were all reasonably fit, we all suffered to varying degrees. Looking at other groups, there didn't seem to be any correlation between fitness and those suffering from altitude sickness.

However this doesn't mean that being fit makes no difference. Climbing Kili is a strenuous activity that involves walking uphill for up to seven hours a day. If you aren't fit you'll struggle regardless of the altitude. It makes sense to have tried something similar before leaving home. Ben Nevis is a good yardstick and actually quite similar, albeit on a vastly different scale – it starts in nice greenery, has some barren middle slopes, involves a climb up scree on the upper slopes and levels off at the top. If you can climb Ben Nevis you are fit enough to climb Kilimanjaro. Ultimately, the fitter you are, the better your chance of being able to cope with whatever is thrown at you, whether that is altitude sickness, a stomach bug or bad weather.

Next up, **are tents or huts better?** The theory is that tents allow you to breathe more fresh air than the huts, and that you should leave your door open overnight (with just the mesh covering closed). This is a difficult one to judge as we only had an opportunity to sample the tents. Sleep is all-important on the climb and you've really got to go for the environment that suits you best. For a couple or two friends, a tent gives you your own space and a quiet place to sleep. I also like camping, so it worked well for me. Huts filled with smelly people going to the toilet all night is not my bag but if you can't sleep well in a tent, maybe it works better for you. Does the extra oxygen that a tent supposedly provides actually make a difference? Again, I think it's the sleep that matters more. I like to sleep with my window open all year round at home, so that works for me. If you like a bit more warmth and a bed, go for the huts.

"Eat a lot of food on the way". Definitely good advice. You are exerting your body more than usual, your body needs more calories than a normal day at the office, so you need to eat more. It's that simple. If you don't, you'll start to feel even more tired than you will from the altitude alone. I'd take more snacks if I went again, to eat on the walks between meals, although we didn't go hungry at any point from not having any. Does altitude reduce your ability to digest food? I'm not sure but it doesn't really matter. Just eat as much as you can at all mealtimes. Can you eat dairy? Almost certainly, although we were not served it for the final climb so I've no way to tell if it would have been a problem.

"Have plenty of spare batteries as they won't last in the cold". Actually, just take good batteries and look after them, and take one spare set as they really aren't that heavy, costly or bulky. I took spare torch batteries and never used them. My headtorch still has the Kili batteries in it and it works fine. I don't have a spare camera battery and that was also fine. In both cases, the appliance itself made a difference. My camera battery lasts for 3 hours of constant use in normal conditions. My headtorch has LED bulbs, meaning it can last for 20 hours of constant use at full brightness. I started the final ascent with both having at least ¾ power left.

"Take as many days as you can to get to the top". While not to be taken too literally, this is sound advice. If we had taken a day less to get to the top, missing out Karranga Huts, for example, then I think all four of us would have really struggled to make it and almost certainly some of us wouldn't have reached the summit. Having extra time to acclimatise really does help. Bearing in mind that every extra day costs money that most of us don't have, a 5 or 6 day trip is usually sufficient.

"Anti-altitude sickness medicines don't help". With all medicines, they work for some people and not for others. Jen took Diamox and she believes it helped stop her vomiting on the lower slopes. I took nothing and never felt particularly nauseous.

"Walk high, sleep low". Probably great advice but your route will almost certainly be pre-planned by your guide and you'll just follow. Often the additional advice is to take an evening stroll to higher ground before returning to your tent to sleep. I didn't and I didn't spot any other evening strollers. In each of our camps except the first, a stroll to anywhere of significant higher altitude would have involved a good half-hour walk that would have clashed with dinner or darkness. We didn't bother.

"Climb at the full moon". No doubt good advice if you can do it. The views of the glacier under moonlight are supposed to be awesome and on the final night you can apparently walk without a headtorch. It wasn't one of our considerations and we spent most of the final night in pitch darkness except for the lit-up boots of the person in front. However, Jen's view is that if she'd been able to see how far we still had to climb to Stellar Point, she'd have probably given up. Only by stubbornly plodding on in the belief that we were almost there did she manage to carry on. So take your pick. We had some great night-time views of the peak along the way under a less-than full moon. Remember that the full moon only helps if it's a cloudless night, so you may want to time your trip for other reasons.

"The porters are just unbelievable!" Indeed they are. They are also human, just like us. They too struggle with the altitude and with carrying heavy loads. They also do it without all the modern equipment that we bring and wear or they carry for us.

We saw porters run past us with huge loads tied with string onto their backs, wearing shorts, t-shirt and flip-flops, and who still flashed us a big grin when we said hello. It's easy to say that this is just their way of life, it's what they are used to and that they are more acclimatised to the conditions. The upper class in Britain used to say similar things about the working class. It was also said about slaves.

Porters don't wear flip-flops because they find them easier to walk in than walking boots. They don't use plastic sheeting to protect them from the rain because it's easier to keep clean. They don't sleep outside because they get more oxygen. They do all these things because they have no choice – they can live with the conditions or not take the work.

If the treatment of porters is your reason for not trekking, think again. The porters and local economy need your money. They just need better conditions as well. Before you choose the tour company that will guide you to the summit, ask them if they follow the International Porter Protection Group's guidelines (available at www.ippg.net). If they've never heard of them, ask to see their porter policy. If they don't have one, find a company that does. The Kilimanjaro Porters Assistance Project (www.kiliporters.org) holds a list of partner organisations dedicated to responsible travel. Having not understood the porter situation until I started writing this book, I was glad to see that the tour company we used was on the list.

My one regret from the climb was that we didn't pay our tip directly to the porters. Limu may have passed on a fair amount to our porters and I do not wish to indicate anything to the contrary. I just don't know it as I did in Peru when the tip was handed individually to each porter.

Last but not least, "**Polè polè!**" Does walking slowly really help? Will you fail if you walk too quickly on the lower slopes? We walked at a reasonable pace and made it to the top. I didn't see any sprinters either fall at the final climb or race past us. The best advice is to walk at a pace for you. Don't be rushed by others if they are fitter or bigger than you are. Also, as in any long-distance endeavour, don't start too quickly and burn out. You wouldn't start a marathon at 100m pace, so don't start climbing Kili as if you'll be there by lunchtime. You have 5 or 6 days of walking ahead, so walk with that in mind. And take time to enjoy the view. The journey is just as good as the destination.

Useless Tat or Essential Kit?
What kit helps and what's superfluous?
Walking poles. These are an absolute necessity for the walk up to the summit and can make the difference between success and failure. We all felt that we wouldn't have made it up the scree to

Stellar Point without them. Maybe the Marangu Route is different in this respect but I doubt it. Whatever, you can hire them in Moshi so if you don't own them, your guide can provide them quite cheaply.

Blow-up air bed. A luxury but excellent if you have one and can spare the space in your rucksack. As I said earlier, sleep is all-important on the climb and anything that can give you that extra few hours is well worth it. We already had three-quarter-length (or nearly full size for Jen!), inch-thick blow-up mats that rolled down very small and we found them to be superb. If you are camping you will be provided with a mat of sorts and it's not awful. You won't need one if you are staying in the huts.

Gaiters. You might look at walkers in the UK wearing these fellers and think they've taken things a bit far, and you might be right. Coming down the scree these are a must. In the forest they keep the mud off your trousers but you've probably got bigger things to worry about. If you don't own a pair, just hire them from your guide.

Down Jacket. I agonised over my decision and was glad I wore one. John and Andy didn't have one and were also fine. Our guide didn't seem to think we needed them. If the weather had been less favourable then I think they would have come into their own, mainly due to the warmth they provide for their size. You can layer up with a thermal and a fleece to achieve something similar and will probably be fine. You can't hire them from your guide. If you normally feel the cold then get one. If not, if you don't have one and if you can't borrow one, I'd save the money as they are easily the most expensive item you might have to buy. Well, alongside a

Four-season sleeping bag. Jen and I had them, John and Andy didn't. They had 3-season bags and coped adequately, although Andy was cold enough to try sleeping in a foil emergency blanket one night. (It didn't work – it made him sweat too much.) Again we had favourable weather. If you have them, take them. If you haven't, you can always sleep in your clothes although I'll say it again, good rest is important. You can't hire them from your guide.

Gloves. You must have two pairs and they must be good quality. I had two pairs: a thermal pair on the inside and a pair of ski-gloves on the outside. My ski gloves were a cheap pair and I suffered for it, by having to hit my hands against my legs to keep them from freezing.

Balaclava, or para-clava as our guides called them. This is a must have. My mum knitted ours, although I used mine as a scarf and wore a wonderfully warm Alpaca hat that was even better. However if it had been raining then the alpaca hat would have been useless and the balaclava essential. The balaclava protects you in two ways – it covers your face from the wind and keeps out the cold. You can hire them from your guide if you don't have one.

Plastic bags. Use them inside your rucksacks to wrap all your kit in. Sitting on top of a porter's head, your bag will get wet if it rains.

Head-torch. You must have one. There are some fantastic and small torches available that use LED lights and last for ages. Mine had a headband that retracted into the torch, making it tiny to carry. It also had the ability to light up a different number of LEDs depending on how bright you want it and how much battery you want to save.

Water-bottles. We all had the camel-packs that sit in your rucksack with a long straw to your mouth. On the lower slopes this is quite handy but not essential, other than it reminds you to drink regularly (which is essential). On the final climb you really don't want to be messing with bottles in your hand, although we had little choice after our water froze. I'm glad I took spare bottles that I kept in my jacket pockets, because they froze last and kept us all hydrated. If you can find a small thermal flask, it will keep some water liquid and you won't regret the extra weight.

Wet wipes. I'm a convert. Having seen dirt and cheese in places I've never seen it before I can't recommend highly enough the splendid job that a large pack of wet-wipes did in keeping my body odour at manageable levels. Jen agrees. Don't leave home without them.

The rest of the kit is the obvious stuff you would need climbing any mountain in Britain in the winter and for overnight stays. Waterproof jacket and trousers, a fleece, good boots, sunglasses, sunhat, high-factor sunblock, your normal toiletries, toilet paper and so on. You'll need a broader range in your first aid kit too. You should take a book to read on the shorter walking days. I'd recommend something a bit more inspirational than my choice.

What made the biggest difference in reaching the summit?

All of the above is about increasing your chances of making it to the top. No one thing will make or break the climb in all circumstances, but the more of it you follow the more likely you are to make it to the top.

Overall, what makes the biggest difference between success and failure? That's easy – the weather. We had fantastic clear skies and no wind, yet our water bottles still froze and I had the beginnings of frostbite. In even slightly less favourable conditions, such as even a mild breeze or rain, things would have been much tougher. In considerably worse conditions, such as strong wind, it would have been impossible. I can now well believe the statistic that only 50% of people make it to the top. On the week we climbed it, I would guess it was more like 80%. Yet there must be plenty of times a year when no-one makes it because the weather doesn't allow it

As for things under your control, the biggest difference is a positive mental attitude combined with respect for the mountain. If you go with the conviction that you'll get to the top then you probably will. If you go happy to get as far as you can, then you'll probably return happy that you got as far as you did. Reaching Uhuru Peak requires a bit of preparation, a bit of fitness and a lot of dogged persistence.

ABOUT THE AUTHOR

Jonathan continues to love the odd scramble up a hill. Jennifer continues to humour him. They now have three sons who share a Pavlovian eye roll at the mention of a short walk.

25944349R00086

Printed in Great Britain
by Amazon